Eight Is Enough

Tom Braden

A FAWCETT CREST BOOK

Fawcett Publications, Inc., Greenwich, Connecticut

To the chief characters portrayed herein, all of whom are actual persons and not to be confused with fictional characters, living or dead.

EIGHT IS ENOUGH

THIS BOOK CONTAINS THE COMPLETE TEXT OF THE ORIGINAL HARDCOVER EDITION.

A Fawcett Crest Book reprinted by arrangement with Random House, Inc.

Copyright © 1975 by Tom Braden

ISBN 0-449-23002-3

Alternate Selection of the Literary Guild, December 1975

Printed in the United States of America

10 9 8 7 6 5 4

CONTENTS

Introduction

When I was a boy in Iowa, my ambition was "to become a pullman conductor and see the world." I know that because I wrote it in a diary I kept when I was seven.

It amuses me now to reflect that my children might have to stop and think before they could tell me what a pullman conductor does. Surely they would smile at the notion that the occupation enables a man "to see the world."

By the time I left Iowa, I had given up the pullman conductor idea and knew I wanted to be a reporter. As it turned out, I was to be a lot of other things too—a printer, soldier, teacher, intelligence officer, publisher and columnist, among other occupations. But it did not occur to me until my own children began to grow up that whenever I fill out those recurrent forms which require a man to state his occupation, I do not tell the whole truth.

7

For the fact is that I spend almost as much of my time and energy and more of my patience and my money on being a father than on the more formal calling with which I describe myself on printed forms. I suspect this is true for other men too, though most do not, as I do, have eight.

Moreover, I doubt that there will ever be an end to my job as a father. I know from looking back that there is no end within a twenty-four-hour day, and as I look ahead, I see no respite during a lifetime. I used to think that when a child was twenty-one, a father's work would be done, but almost any father of a twenty-one-year-old will tell you that's not true. The process of maturing has grown longer at the same time that the law has cut it down. Maybe the farm boys of the generation before mine were men at eighteen, but does any father have an eighteen-year-old son of whom he would honestly say, "That boy is fully mature"?

A daughter? More likely. But any father who makes such a claim for an eighteen-year-old daughter ought to be able to pass the following test:

Has he stayed up late on any night this past week muttering to himself about where the hell she is?

Has his wife complained recently about missing articles of clothing, toiletry or jewelry?

Have there been any unwelcome surprises in the mail: library fines; notices of an increase in automobile insurance; charges at the department store?

Unless the father of an eighteen-year-old daughter can answer all three questions in the negative, he has not finished his job. Not yet.

And I have not finished mine. I won't be able to finish it for a long time, because although I have a son who is twenty-three, I also have a son who is nine. Even if I thought that the twenty-three-year-old was all he should be, I would still have to figure on fourteen years.

In between the twenty-three-year-old and the nine-year-old, there are a lot of others. Let me list the children for you, starting at the top, because they comprise the chief characters of this book and if you read it, you may want to refer back now and then to see who these people are now and how old they are as compared to who they were and how old they were at the times they enter the story.

David is twenty-three. He has red hair, great strength in his arms and quickness of foot. For a long time, it did not seem to me that he changed his shirt often enough. I think he got very tired of hearing about this and that may be the reason why he went off recently to Alaska and got a job as a guard in a prison. In his last letter he wrote that he has also enrolled in a college, and this surprised and pleased me so much that it brought about a change of image. When I think of him now, he is wearing a clean shirt.

Mary is twenty-one. When she was a baby, one of her feet was turned a little inward, and the doctor said to rub it. I spent a lot of time rubbing that foot, outward, and while I was doing it, I made up a song about her, a very sentimental and sweet song such as one might sing to a baby. It would greatly embarrass her if I sang it now. But I will if I have to.

Mary is a junior at college; studious, thoughtful, good-looking, and left-wing. I am reserving the song as the ultimate weapon. If the era of campus demonstrations should return and Mary should again feel it necessary to take a leading part, I shall go to her school, approach her while she is in the act of protesting the system, and sing that song. Her foot, incidentally, is just fine.

Joannie is twenty. Very bright-eyed. She enjoys life more than most people because she pays more attention to it. "For Saturday breakfast," she wrote me recently, "we made 'fried bread.' A whole plate in the middle of the table; before each place a bowl of maple syrup. Just close your eyes and imagine the delight. Later I tried skiing straight across the golf course. Then it began to snow, so I read about Hamilton and Burr in front of a fire. I love Saturdays."

Few people, it seems to me, are able to observe and reflect while maintaining full speed. But Joannie does.

Susan is nineteen and a sophomore at college. She works very hard and plays very hard and regards each hour as a frame in which much must be done: From six in the morning until seven is the time to get up, run two miles and eat breakfast. From seven until eight, one studies a language; from eight until nine, one washes dishes at the college cafeteria or cleans the kitchen when at home. The rest of the day is similarly divided into hourly duties. Susan hardly ever speaks, either of duty or anything else. She has light-brown hair and large, sloe eyes. A fine athlete, she bats right and throws left.

Nancy is eighteen. As a baby and a little girl, she early developed the habit of taking her clothes off as fast as they were put on, so that she earned the nickname "Barechild." But now that she is grown into a tall, voluptuous and rather languorous blonde, we are embarrassed to call her that any more. Nancy is very bright but is nevertheless having a love affair.

Elizabeth is fifteen. Long red hair, graceful, high tempered, with a habit of tossing her head in disdain, and of large spirit. Elizabeth has a great many freckles and for many years was the subject of a popular family song entitled "Too many freckles." But like Nancy's sobriquet, the song has now been relegated to history, for it turned out as Elizabeth grew into an astonishingly pretty girl, that it was not so.

Tommy is thirteen, with blond hair and a mouthful of braces. Wise for his years and rabbinical in his garb, he wears both in and out of doors a large and nondescript stocking cap. A mine of accurate information on starting line-ups, he sees life as a personal combat. Witness his definition of the word "evidence" as I found it on a school paper, graded "B":

"If for breakfast, two people have eggs and

one person leaves and when he comes back his egg is gone and there is egg all over the other guy's face, that is evidence, though it is not proven."

Nicholas is nine and often has egg on his face. He also has mischievous eyes, and it is perhaps the look in Nicholas' eyes that Tommy regards as proof. In any event, Nicholas gets beaten up more than anybody I know and, considering this, he remains remarkably cheerful and fun to be with.

In addition, there is a person named Joan who is the mother of all these children and who is an extraordinarily capable, bright, lively and good-looking girl.

All these people live in or come home to a big yellow house in Maryland which has sufficient bedrooms and a yard and food in the refrigerator.

Also, the house nearly always holds and often sleeps a number of friends, some of whom you will meet in the pages that follow. If the names of some of the friends are familiar to you, you must consider that my job is writing a newspaper column from Washington and therefore a lot of the people I know are known by many other people too.

Inside the house with all these children, the well-known people behave just like other people, discussing with the children the problems of state and the problems of children. On the latter subject I have found them generally supportive of a father's point of view.

Well-known or not, no one who visits the big

yellow house would, I think, dispute my contention that after the word "occupation," I ought to write "father."

How I Resigned As a Father

It gives me great pleasure to look back upon the time that I resigned as a father. Solemnly, I handed the eight children what remained of their eight airline tickets. Solemnly, I bade them farewell.

We were nearing the end of that ghastly Christmas trip to the Caribbean, and I had had plenty of time to think the resignation through. So there was nothing angry about it; no bluster, no threats, no demands.

But I have never been able to decide which event in that whole series of events, each more exasperating and demeaning than the last—which event was it that forced me to the final step. And how did it start? Did it start, as resignations so often do, with doubt? Was it the sinking doubt I felt as I heard my wife say, "I'll pay the difference"?

Joan frequently offers to "pay the difference,"

and it is a sincere and generous offer because Joan is a sincere and generous girl. She buys her own clothes with the money she earns and always has some left over to be generous with. But what she has left over would be spent ten, nay a hundred, times if she indeed were required to pay the difference as she so often says she will.

Joan never worries about money. She is constantly and quite genuinely astonished that I should be worried about it. In moments of deep gloom, when I predict poverty or ask how she thinks we're going to live when we're old, she replies, "How do you know you'll be old?"

So when it comes to something everybody in the family wants to have or to do, I'm the one who says, "We can't afford it," and Joan is the one who says, "I'll pay the difference." Usually I reply with an appropriate snort. But sometimes, as on this Christmas occasion, I relent.

We were having an argument about taking eight children to the Caribbean for Christmas. Joan thought it would be a bargain. To stay at home and have Christmas presents for everyone, she contended, would cost about the same as to take everyone to the Caribbean, with the understanding that the trip would be the present; no others to be purchased; no others to be anticipated.

To buttress her position and to give it authority, as well as class, she had consulted, over a cocktail and a wafer, Chairman of the Federal Reserve Board Arthur Burns, or at least she told me she had. And I didn't doubt it, for Joan and Arthur

Burns are friends, and Arthur Burns, a kindly and pleasant man, might well have agreed with Joan that she could do whatever it was she wanted to do.

Braving the contrary opinion of Burns, I tried arithmetic. "Ten airplane tickets at one hundred and fifty is fifteen hundred. Plus, say, five hundred for the motel. Have we ever spent two thousand dollars on Christmas presents?"

"Closer to a thousand," she admitted, "but you're not counting the tree and the decorations and a big dinner and guests and bringing in help. Anyhow, I'll pay the difference."

I recall a sense of foreboding, not only about what the difference would be, but about Joan's ability to pay it. Was that the first ingredient in the amalgam of anger, weakness and inability to cope which resignation implies?

Or was it Pan American Airlines? "We won't be able to get all of you on," said the man behind the counter as I handed over the ten tickets shortly before departure time. My jaw dropped. "What?" "That's right, sir. We have seven available seats but I may be able to find one more." He was businesslike. "Just wait till I finish counting." He bent over a huge chart. "Jim, did you say 230 or 231?"

My mind raced back over the morning: the five-thirty rising, the cup of coffee brought to my wife in bed by her namesake child, Joannie; the two taxis; the fourteen bags; the enforced jettisoning of the inevitable odd paper bags full of gum and dolls which always turn up at the front door whenever we go any place; the resultant tears; the trip back to the house because six-year-old Nicholas had to go to the bathroom; the airport; the tips; the fourteen bags again.

And now, what had the man said? "We won't be able to get all of you on." I was thunderstruck. Before my mind's eye, there flashed a picture of my friend Stewart Alsop, the *Newsweek* columnist, practicing his technique of a "puce face." Confronted by outrageous conduct on the part of those who are engaged in the business of serving the public, Alsop would inhale deeply until his lungs and cheeks were fully extended. He would then hold his breath while at the same time jumping in place, on both feet. The sealed-in air, combined with exertion, caused the face to turn bright red and the eyes to bulge. The room clerk who had sold out his hotel reservation, or the ticket agent who had presided over the surrender of his seat often assumed that he was dealing with a man about to have a stroke. Often, he would yield. I thought of making a puce face.

But Joan had beaten me to the tactic of demonstration. First, she screamed; then she began to cry. It was not going to do any good. The man behind the counter adopted that air of wounded patience so necessary to employees of airlines which regularly oversell their space and seldom get caught except at Christmas. "Take the seven seats, Mr. Braden, or I'll have to put the standbys on."

Behind me a sea of faces pressed forward eagerly, eyes estimating the chances if I should decide to spurn an offer of less than that to which I was entitled. Joan was still crying and I could hear sentences between the sobs. "I made these reservations two months ago; I reconfirmed them yesterday." The moment had come. Quickly, I counted off the children according to age, separated the baggage according to ownership, and ordered seven—Joan and the six youngest—across the barrier. The two oldest and I would arrive a day late.

It was maddening; it was abject; it was unfair; it was more than inconvenient; it was destructive of joy and of the pride of family. It was also fate, proving that I was a fool ever to have consented to this nonessential, expensive and exhausting expedition. But it was not a moment of resignation. I did not flag or fail. I sat in the airport all that day and halfway into the night and tried to be cheerful the while. It never occurred to me to bug out.

In fact, I do not believe that the thought of bugging out actually crossed my mind until Christmas was over and the trip home was well under way, and we were at an airport again and I had counted the fourteen bags again and handed the ten tickets over again, and the man had said, "Go right on board, Mr. Braden," and I looked around and five of the party weren't there.

I was panic-stricken. There was no time to lose. "They went to the restaurant with Nancy," one of the loyalists volunteered. Quickly, I strode through tables and chairs; quickly, I collared Nancy, who is sixteen and has long blond hair and blue jeans; quickly, I dragged her and her fellow deserters aboard. People looked up from their eggs. "It was embarrassing," Nancy said later, and I suppose it was. But I found her defense maddening. "After all," she explained to her mother, when she found her seat and the engines were starting, "I was spending my own money."

The other children sided with her. And Joan said she could see two sides. Two sides! Maybe that was the moment of decision. But if I was maddened, irritated, angry at Nancy's "own money" or at my wife's seeing "two sides," the last straw, the thing that drove me up the wall, was the remark about the platoon leader.

It was two-thirty in the morning and I was standing outside the elevator on the eighth floor of a hotel at John F. Kennedy International Airport. I had supervised the loading of the fourteen bags from the conveyor belt and helped carry them to the bus and into the lobby, and now they were scattered in front of me and I was mentally trying to assign them and ten people into three double rooms with cots in two. "Dad," said my daughter Mary, with that air of supreme superiority which only college sophomores attain, "You act as though you were some kind of platoon leader. Don't you think running things as though we were all in the army is a little bit, shall I say, old-fashioned?" Her eyebrows arched and her lips pursed the final words.

That was the moment; that must have been the moment. "How else?" I said to myself, "how else do you get ten people to the Caribbean and back?

How else do you hassle their baggage, count their tickets, parcel out their passports, pay their head taxes, get them out of restaurants and onto airplanes? How else, but by being a platoon leader? An honorable post, platoon leader. I have been a platoon leader once in my life and at no time during my tenure in that office did I have to put up with this kind of thing."

It was about nine that morning that I resigned.

How Everything Became Unwieldy

Probably I should never have had eight children. It seems odd to reflect that as recently as ten years ago, large families were not frowned upon. My mother was one of seven; my father the youngest of thirteen. Today, according to the Census Bureau, the average American family has 2.2 children. It is not only no longer fashionable to be polyphiloprogenitive; it is considered a positive crime against the environment. I understand this. I agree with the felt need, and I remember very well when it first occurred to me that eight was, if not too many, at least enough.

We were lying in bed in Oceanside, California, where I ran a newspaper, and Joan was nursing Nicholas, our eighth child. First we had had a boy, and then we'd had five girls, and though I never admitted to myself that I had a sex bias, the arrival of Elizabeth, the fifth girl, had seemed, at the time, redundant.

But an odd thing happened. Elizabeth turned out to have red hair, which made her very different. And then had come Tommy and then Nicholas. Stub Harvey, who was my golfing and touch football partner as well as the family doctor, pronounced the odds: "From now on you'll have boys."

Anyhow, on that morning the mail had come, brought to us in bed by one of the children, and Joan, opening it, paused over a telegram and laughed out loud. "Wonderful," she said, passing it on to me. With the tolerance due a mother with a newborn son, I refrained from remarking that it was addressed to me.

It was signed by the Attorney General of the United States, Robert F. Kennedy. "Congratulations," it read, "I surrender."

I was amused and proud. How many did the Kennedys have? Seven? But then a horrifying thought struck me. How much money did the Kennedys have? Somewhere I had read that each of the children of the Attorney General's generation had been made several times a millionaire. What was I doing accepting congratulations from a Kennedy on having more children than a Kennedy? Eight, it seemed to me at that moment, was enough.

It was, as I recall, my first major doubt and as it grew into decision, the Kennedys remained helpful. For example, I remember one summer in Aspen, Colorado, where we used to take the children from time to time, camping high. One morning, before the expedition was to start, Susan, who was ten, came into the motel bedroom bearing coffee for her mother and a copy of the Denver *Post*. I noticed that she was excited as she watched over the brimming cup she held in outstretched hand. "Mom," she said, "a terrible thing has happened. The Kennedys have caught up."

There it was, a small squib on the front page. "Number Eight for Ethel." Unanimously, the children urged that I do something about it at once. Joan thought it was funny. I pretended to laugh, but inwardly, I had made a resolution.

Was this joke about rivalry with the Kennedys transformed, in the minds of the children, into real rivalry, even animosity? On a subsequent summer, the Kennedy family also turned up in Aspen, and Bobby and Ethel and Joan and I all went out to the movies, leaving the Kennedy and Braden children in a rented house. When we came home, we found that the Braden children had locked themselves inside the house and were holding it as a fort while the Kennedys stood outside in the dark, some throwing rocks as cover while others made periodic assaults in an effort to storm the doors.

Looking back now, I'd like to pretend that it was all very friendly, which was, of course, what we pretended at the time. But it was not friendly. Those rocks were real. Do large families develop intense tribal loyalty and more than average consciousness of turf? Are they, therefore, inclined to be quarrelsome and aggressive when as a tribe they are placed in proximity to another tribe of relatively equal strength or self-esteem?

I had not liked that moment in the dark with the rocks flying. Too many rocks. Too many children.

But that was in 1963. It was not until late in 1966 that resolution turned to embarrassment and that I realized I could be charged with being an over-consumer of the world's goods.

"You're his type of guy," Kirk Douglas had said, speaking of Charlton Heston. "He ought to come in for at least a thousand." Douglas was having a fund-raising party, and the funds were for me because I was running for lieutenant governor of California. Kirk had been a stalwart in my campaign and that afternoon he had packed his house with friends and acquaintances and made the money pitch. Then, while the hat was being passed, Kirk brought Heston over to a corner of the room for a private chat; just Heston and me. Heston broke the ice with the subject of planned parenthood and we never got off it. He was, it turned out, an ardent advocate, a committed committee man. He told me how he had enlisted in the battle against population growth. The figures which proved the soundness of the cause came readily to his mind. Sometime during the conversation, he pulled out a check and wrote on it, holding it against the wall, and when he departed, he handed it, folded, to me. Not until I had turned it over to Kirk and saw the disappointment on his face did I remember that at one point the conversation had taken a personal turn.

"A hundred dollars," Kirk announced flatly.

Then, "What in the hell did you say to him?"

"He only asked me one question," I replied. "I told him I had eight."

I still do have eight. I was reminded of it only yesterday. I had to write a column, get started on the income tax, do a radio broadcast, and have lunch with the Indian Ambassador. In addition, there were a lot of telephone calls. About 7 P.M. I settled into a brown leather chair to have a drink with my wife and review events. The following had occurred:

1. Joan had been called at her office in the early afternoon to be notified that Elizabeth was at the police station.

2. Mary had not eaten since her arrival from college for a brief vacation three days previously. Joan explained that she had become a Buddhist and was fasting.

3. Tommy's teacher had called to say that he was doing well at baseball but paying no attention to classroom activity and would we please exercise influence?

4. There was a nice letter from David, who was traveling around the world and had reached Afghanistan. The mail also included a notice from the American Express Company acknowledging the loss of his traveler's checks.

5. Joannie had backed the station wagon into the stone pillar at the end of the driveway. Estimated damage: $150.00.

6. We had an inconclusive discussion about what to do about Nancy, whom Joan described as "in a state of rebellion." Would we confront

her, risking defiance? Or should we leave her out of family plans and hope she cared?

The problem of Elizabeth and the police station had been solved. At least, she was now in her room. It had been a warm day; she had skipped school and gone window shopping and a policeman had noticed. Should I go to her now, while I still think it's serious, or should I wait and risk revealing that I know she's not the first truant in history?

As I say, Joan and I were discussing these problems when Nicholas skipped excitedly into the room. "Dad," he said, "tonight's the finals of the basketball tournament and you promised to watch with me." I looked shamefacedly at Joan. She broke the news. "Daddy and I have to go out to dinner."

When Nicholas had left, I remarked gently, "Maybe we have too many children."

"You're wrong," Joan replied. "We just don't have enough time."

Why We Had Eight

I know how I had children. The same way everybody has children. But eight is different. And the difference was Joan.

The first time I ever saw the girl, I was sitting in the outer office of Nelson A. Rockefeller, waiting for an interview. I had been teaching at Dartmouth College, and one day the President of Dartmouth, an ebulliently kind and interested man named John Dickey, asked me if I would like to talk to his friend, Nelson Rockefeller, about a job at the Museum of Modern Art. I don't think John Dickey was trying to get rid of me. I think he thought I was too much interested in too many things to be interested forever in teaching English to college freshmen.

So there I was in Nelson Rockefeller's outer office. I remember the magazine I looked up from. *Business Week*. I haven't read *Business Week* very often in the years that have passed but I have always honored its name.

So I looked up and there was a girl in a dark-green taffeta dress with a skirt that sort of swirled, and she had a marvelously fresh and open face and freckles and curly, brown hair. She was the prettiest girl I had ever seen in my life.

The mating rites have changed a lot since then, so I am told. Women have adopted what was once the man's role. They no longer lure, they suggest; at times they attack; they no longer wait for the light to be dimmed, they dim it; or even don't care if it's dimmed. A great emancipation is at work. I'm sure women feel less unnaturally subservient and men less unnaturally responsible and uptight. But it all came too late for me. Joan had never called a man on the telephone in her life. She still won't do it. I had to be the aggressor, and when I think about the aggression, I think of its symbol. Without doubt, I should say, it was Joan's skirt.

I've seen Joan in a lot of skirts, and I've bought a lot of them. There was the taffeta skirt she wore that day in Rockefeller's office, and the blue and purple plaid skirt that I bought for her in Scotland that first summer after we were married. Once I bought her a dress in Paris off the back of a model who was almost as pretty as she was. On the model, the bodice was transparent. I wasn't used to buying clothes from models and it was embarrassing. I wouldn't let Joan wear it with the bodice transparent, but the way other people looked at her when she wore that dress, she might as well have. The dress was around the house for a long while. When did I last see it, faded now, and no longer crisp, but still beautiful? I remember. Elizabeth wore it last Halloween.

What was it about Joan? What is sexy? Was it a good figure? Was it that she blushed? Was it that she was so pretty? You'd have to work very hard not to have babies if you were married to Joan.

But I'm capable of hard work, so why didn't I work hard not to have babies? At least, not to have eight babies? Was it simply that people tend to behave within the bounds of societal permission, and that when Joan and I were having babies, society had not yet signaled that we shouldn't?

There were accidents. Two of the children were accidents. That's twenty-five percent. But when I think back to the days before the pill and all that harness and hardware, is it any wonder people had accidents? Maybe twenty-five percent of all Americans over twenty are accidents.

Money must have had something to do with eight children. We never had enough money but we always had just enough, or thought we would have. As everybody knows, babies don't cost much until they're not babies any more.

Then there was the electricity factor. Eugene Black, who used to be the head of the World Bank, once told me that the best way to cut down population growth in the underdeveloped countries was to install electricity. Far better than dispensing birth control information. Joan and

I lived on the beach in Oceanside, California, and though the town had plenty of electricity, the electricity factor was nevertheless at work.

Two theaters there were, showing movies almost exclusively aimed at the young men who lived nearby on the Marine Corps base at Camp Pendleton. So what to do at night? In Oceanside it was either a movie or the PTA meeting.

So I get back to the skirt. President Kennedy was coming down the White House steps to take Joan to a car one evening after a Halloween party with his daughter Caroline and my daughter, Susan, and suddenly he noticed something and he said to Joan, "Again?"

And she said, "Yes, again."

And he remarked, "Why don't you get Tom tied?"

I never knew a girl who looked prettier in a skirt nor one who so unconsciously and yet so irresistibly flaunted before my eyes the challenge to take it off.

That's the reason we had eight children. The skirt. The rest is persiflage.

How to Have Babies

Having babies was very difficult for me at first, but it got a whole lot easier with practice. The hardest baby was the second one, and I remember the occasion with shame because I lost my temper and swore at my wife. "How could I have done that?" I ask myself even now, and the answer comes back: "For the same reason you always lose your temper: when you have done something stupid, and want to blame it on somebody else."

It was early in the morning—which is when babies nearly always come—and I was not a bit nervous when Joan awakened me to tell me she was having pains. After all, everything was in readiness. When you're counting on a baby, you have to plan carefully. You have to have the doctor's number by the bedside; you have to have your clothes ready to slip into; you have to tell your wife to let you know the moment she feels any pains; you have to have the car full of gas; you have to stay alert. No drinking after dinner.

Indeed, I had planned for this moment so carefully that on the table by the bed I had placed, along with the doctor's number, a thin volume in hardcover, with a pinkish jacket, entitled *Childbirth*. I had read it through and noted its specific instructions on every aspect of the event.

So when Joan spoke, I switched on the light and picked up *Childbirth* at once. Joan described the pains in detail. They turned out to be not so much pains as twitches. I turned to *Childbirth*'s last chapter. Sure enough, *Childbirth* described the twitches. I began to read out loud, Joan lying beside me in a ruffled blue and white nightgown. With gratification, I remarked on finding her symptoms so precisely mirrored on the pages in front of me. And then I came to the last sentence. "My God," I exclaimed, "it says here '. . . in any case, call the doctor.'" *Childbirth* had left the most important instruction for the very end. I sprang from the bed, called the doctor and hurried into my clothes.

Joan dressed more leisurely. She always does, but on this occasion it seemed to me she was more deliberate than usual, demonstrating a meticulous care for the selection of each item of clothing or bottle of lotion which was to go into the overnight bag that had lain so long by the bathroom door.

I started the car and let it run, then went back to get the overnight bag, led Joan to the car, and swung out the driveway and down the road.

The gas gauge on the Chevrolet had registered empty for a long time and I remarked to Joan as we looked into the black dawn that it gave me a queasy feeling, "Even though I know it's full."

"Well, it can't be quite full," she said casually. "What do you mean?" I asked, turning to look at her in surprise. "I had it filled night before last and it's been sitting in the driveway ever since." "No," she answered calmly. "The Crowes borrowed it yesterday for house hunting and brought it back last night just before you came home from the office." I was appalled. "You can't do this kind of thing to me," I said. "Why do you suppose I haven't been taking the car to the office? So you'd be able to get to the hospital or so that you could lend it to the Crowes?"

But Joan was on her way to have a baby. I told myself, "Gently now." There was nothing to do but to suppose that the Crowes did not drive very far, or that, if they did, they had had the courtesy to replenish the tank. But I feared the worst. My care had gone for naught; my forethought had been unavailing. It seemed to me that the car sputtered.

I stopped for a red light. It was beginning to get lighter and a few blocks away, I could make out the hospital with its wide circular driveway. The light changed and I put my foot on the pedal. Nothing happened. I pressed the starter button. Again, nothing. We had stalled. "God damn it," I said. "God damn you and God damn the Crowes. We're out of gas and we're about to have a baby and you have treated this whole thing as though it were some nonserious, casual affair."

I looked at Joan. There were two tears running down her left cheek. The twitches had turned into pains. She was having to be brave.

I pressed the starter button hard. It ground fruitlessly. I got out of the car, turned the steering wheel sharply to the right and pushed toward the curb, swearing breathlessly. And by the curb I left it. There was nothing else to do. I ushered Joan out of the curbside door, and started walking gently and with small steps, but quickly. With firm application of my arm against her back, we proceeded the four blocks toward the hospital.

Dr. Brown, a man with curly black hair, was waiting in the driveway, wearing a white jacket. He was obviously disturbed. He called for a wheelchair and hurried Joan down the long hall toward the elevators. I went to the front desk and filled out forms.

It seemed to me that everybody was particularly kindly and helpful. Nurses put scrubbed fingers at the places where I was to sign and exercised great care in their directions about where I was to go next. I didn't get quite which way it was that I was to turn to reach the elevator nor the floor where I would find Joan. "Did you say six or seven?" I asked. A nurse said sweetly, "Come with me, Mr. Braden, and I'll show you." I think people thought I was nervous and distracted. But I was not conscious of being so. The nurse put me on the elevator and I found the right floor and the right desk to ask at, and Dr. Brown appeared from somewhere to tell me that the baby was already born. It was a girl. He said it had been a close call. "We didn't even have time to prepare her. But there's no point in your staying here. Why don't you go out and get something to eat and come back in a couple of hours when she'll be awake?"

So I went out and walked down the street to the car, thinking about Joan and the baby. It was a bright fall morning now, and I was a very solid fellow. We had had a boy baby, and this time we had wanted a girl baby. So we got a girl baby. That's the way it was, I reflected, with Joan and with me.

When I got to the car, I didn't even think about the fact that it was illegally parked. Certainly I never thought about the gas. I just got in and started up and drove straight home.

How Not to Have Babies

When a man has eight children, a lot of things tend to run together in his mind. I mean, I can never remember how old each of the children is, or the dates of their births.

But I remember very well the birthdays themselves—a bright and beautiful day in June when the leaves were still fresh and the azaleas were in bloom. That was the day Joannie was born. After that, there was a day in May, which was cold, as I well remember, because with Joan doing all that had to be done inside the hospital, I fixed subconsciously upon a compensatory activity.

I parked the car outside the hospital and got buckets of water from a nearby filling station and bought a sponge and washed the car. It takes just about as long to wash a car by hand as it does for Joan to have a baby. That was Susan's birthday. But the day I remember best, a much colder and gloomier day, was the day Elizabeth was born. Everything about that day was full of ugly portent, as though on Julius Caesar's ides of March, a lioness had whelped upon the street.

It was not Joan's fault that Elizabeth was the fifth girl in a row and it was not Elizabeth's fault. Besides, I was not really depressed that she was the fifth girl in a row and I liked the bright red hair I saw on the top of her head. And yet, the whole event seemed irritating and tense; I paced the floor in nervous desperation as Joan and I chatted, until at last she said, "Why don't you just go home?"

I think Joan had the impression that she had been a failure. I had said something offhand as I bent down to kiss her. "Gee, another girl." It was not the thing to say. You have to be very careful about Joan when she has a baby. You have to say that it is the most beautiful baby ever born, even more beautiful than the last. And that the baby has the most beautiful mother. You have to say the nightgown Joan is wearing and which she has bought especially for the occasion is a particularly beautiful nightgown, and you have to say it in such a manner as to suggest that you wish to get into bed with her at once, which of course, you don't, knowing how weak and sort of dopey from Demerol she is, and seeing that tiny, vulnerable thing lying there alongside. What if you rolled over on it? It's a sexless moment but you have to pretend it isn't—that is, unless you want Joan to burst into tears.

Which is exactly what she did on this occasion and with every good reason. I was, as she said, "cross." I was abrupt; I paced the floor; I said things like "Well, I guess I better go now."

This last was particularly insensitive. Joan and I had a thing we always did in honor of newborn babies. We always had dinner together in the hospital room for as long as she was there. The first night, it was something I went out and got for myself to eat. On the first night, Joan ate the hospital's food, whatever the doctor ordered. But after that, the meals got better. Nothing from the hospital, that was our rule. I would go out to a good store and buy things fit to eat—things like sliced roast beef and homemade bread and consommé, which I would take home and then bring fresh from the refrigerator. Sometimes I would buy half a bottle of champagne, and once, a tiny tin of caviar. We made a party out of having babies.

But not with Elizabeth. I said, "I guess I'd better go now," and Joan cried, not loudly nor complainingly, but softly and all alone.

I know now why I was the way I was—nervous and impatient and unable to sit down or think about anything for very long, even about staying in one place for very long. It was because I had stopped smoking.

A man should never stop smoking when he is having a baby. The effect upon him is nothing out of the ordinary; the well-known list of tortures: inability to relax; inability to work; inability to carry on a consecutive conversation; temper tantrums; loss of self-confidence; shyness; constipation; a tendency to acne . . . But these are nothing to the effect which stopping smoking has upon a man's wife. I was not myself, and so Joan was not herself and as a result, the birth and the first few days of the life of Elizabeth were traumatic.

At first, I did not know how traumatic they were. Only Joan knew, and she had been exposed to knowledge I did not have. Until shortly before Elizabeth was born, Joan had been serving on one of those essentially decorative government commissions which abound in Washington and which afford free travel and hotel rooms for the hinterland laity to visit their capital city and "advise." Before we moved from Washington to California, Joan had been executive assistant to the first Secretary of Health, Education and Welfare, a bright and beautiful woman named Oveta Culp Hobby. When Joan resigned, Mrs. Hobby appointed her as one of the public members of the Neurological Advisory Board of the National Institutes of Health.

This is not the place for a critique of the system by which the government pays people who know nothing about a subject to come to Washington to hear about it from those who do. Maybe the system of public membership on scientific Boards is the edifice which we Americans erect to our faith in the common sense of the people. Joan did not know anything about neurological diseases, nor, to the best of my observations, did any of her fellow public members on the Neurological Board. But four times a year they came to Washington to hear doctors who did know about neurology tell them why they wanted to spend their money the way they wanted to spend it and why they needed more.

It was at one of these meetings, the most recent one, that Joan heard a lecture and was shown pictures of how children behaved when they had such diseases. She says she told me about this—described it in detail—not only before Elizabeth was born, but afterward and often. My attention must have been elsewhere. If you want to get the attention of a man who has stopped smoking, you have to say or do something unusual. And Joan finally did.

At three one morning, during that first week after she got home from the hospital, I awoke to hear the sound of bare feet pacing up and down the long hall outside our bedroom door. Joan was carrying Elizabeth in her arms and crying. I called gently from the bed. "Anything wrong?" No answer. Standing now in the hall in my pajamas, and blinking at the light, I asked again, "What's the matter?"

Joan was walking slowly up and down, the tears pouring down her cheeks. As she reached the point where I stood blocking the hallway, she suddenly pressed herself against me, and I held her tight. "There's no cure," she said softly, "there's no cure for cerebral palsy." The thought struck like a blow and somewhere deep under my stomach, the blow hurt. I disentangled myself, holding Joan out at arm's length so I could look at her. "Cerebral palsy?" I repeated. "What about cerebral palsy?" "Look," she replied. She held the baby out before her at arm's length. It was a very tiny baby with red fringe over the ears and a very light red fuzz on top of the head; and the moment she was held straight out before her mother, her head fell forward.

I stood there under the bright bulbs in the hallway and tried to be calm and sensible. I took the baby from Joan and held her in my arms. She was sleepy but did not cry, and I patted her gently. Then, ever so softly and slowly, I moved my right hand downward from the back of her neck as she lay in my arms and, taking her with both hands at the waist, I held her out in front of me. At once, the head fell forward . . . Joan looked at me, forlorn and suddenly seeming very small and defenseless in her new nightgown. "You see?" was all she said.

It was necessary to take hold. Bluster is better than crying. "Now, look," I said, "this is nonsense. I don't know a damned thing about cerebral palsy and I don't think you're an expert after one lecture and a movie. Get to bed. Get to bed right now." "I'm going to call Dr. Harvey," Joan replied. "No," I said. "It's four o'clock in the morning and there's nothing he can do about it now. Get to bed."

I lay down and touched my feet to hers, which I always do because her feet are always cold. For a long time we lay there, not talking. Then Joan spoke, in a whisper. "Tom, what if she does?" I sat upright in bed. "We forget about her," I answered. "We put her somewhere and we never go back and look. She was never in our life until four days ago, and if she has cerebral palsy, she never will be in our life. Now quit worrying about it and go to sleep and we'll find out in the morning."

It was a dreadful thing to say about Elizabeth, now that I look back on it, and not a very bright thing to say to Joan at the time. I don't think either one of us slept. At eight, I called Dr. Harvey. "I think you're talking a lot of foolishness. That's the kind of thing I'd have noticed. But bring her over now."

So, there we were in the tiny office and Stub took the baby and held her out in front of him and her head fell forward and he laughed out loud, turning his bright, twinkling eyes upon us as we stood there watching. "What did you think? You have to hold a baby's head. Elizabeth hasn't got enough muscle to hold it straight up all by herself. Joan, you're tired. I'm going to give you some quiet pills." Then, turning to me: "I don't know what's the matter with you. After six babies, you ought to know more about babies' necks than you do."

Elizabeth is fifteen now and has a fine neck, which I notice once in a while when she pins her red hair up high just to show off or to look grown up. She always carries her head very high and it is a singular mark of gracefulness in this singularly graceful girl.

So there was never anything wrong with Elizabeth and never anything really wrong with Joan. A new mother is entitled to unnecessary worry, to periods of depression, even to hallucination.

I was the one who was wrong. I had disturbed
her peace by the way I had behaved in the hospital. Sometimes when I think about Elizabeth
I feel guilty and am glad that I can blame my
conduct on the fact that I had stopped smoking.

Animals I Have Known

In the spring of 1974 the Supreme Court of the United States upheld, in the case of Village of Belle Terre v. Boraas, a zoning ordinance on Long Island. Rather surprisingly, the majority opinion was written by William O. Douglas, who had for several years usually been heard in dissent.

I do not "reach," as judges say, the merits of the Douglas opinion, which ordered six students in Belle Terre to vacate a one-family dwelling on the grounds that they were not, in the words of the town's ordinance, "related to each other by blood, adoption or marriage."

But there were some words in Mr. Justice Douglas' opinion which made me wonder whether this extraordinarily conservative view was wholly unrelated to his experience with Elizabeth's sheep.

Mr. Justice Douglas was sitting in our dining room one summer evening having dinner when suddenly the door opened and in came Elizabeth's sheep. The sheep came straight for Justice Douglas, nudged him a little, and then, brushing hard by, got under the table in front of his chair, folded his legs front first, and stiffly, as sheep do, lay down under his feet.

I think Mr. Justice Douglas was surprised, but he evinced no displeasure and nobody said anything about it except Elizabeth, who remarked that the sheep's name was Worthy.

However, the Justice later commented upon the encounter in conversation with friends, and remarked upon the singular fact that the sheep's entrance had gone unchallenged. He called it—and I think he called it accurately—"strange."

I remember the incident well and I recall my extreme annoyance when Worthy walked into the room. But I knew better than to try to do anything about it. I don't know how long it had been since Mr. Justice Douglas dealt with a sheep. Once in a dining room, a sheep is exceedingly difficult to dislodge. A sheep does not come when called, will not take directions by gesture, is fast and clever at dodging, and if caught, can adopt a virtually immovable stance.

My point is that the reason nobody in the family said anything when Worthy got under Mr. Douglas' feet was that everybody knew there was nothing to do. To try to get Worthy out of the room while the table was laid—and with the good tablecloth Joan had bought in Ireland reaching to just above the floor where Worthy lay—would have made a scene much worse than that which

Mr. Douglas had witnessed and perhaps more disruptive than judicial temperament might tolerate.

So we said nothing and did nothing, and I can see why the Justice thought it was "strange."

Anyhow, in the case of the Village of Belle Terre v. Boraas, Mr. Douglas—joined for the first time in many a month by unaccustomed concurrences from such as Burger, C. J.; Blackmun, Powell and Rehnquist—spoke approvingly of the police power to lay out places where, as he put it, "the blessings of quiet seclusion . . . make a sanctuary . . ."

Then came the clincher. The Justice quoted: "'A nuisance may be merely a right thing in the wrong place—like a pig in the parlor instead of the barnyard!'"

It was vivid, almost explosive language for an opinion of the Court and maybe it is only lingering embarrassment which suggests that the author of the opinion may have had a sheep under the dinner table in mind.

Worthy was named from the Bible, and if there was sacrilege in the name, it was at least exact. For Worthy was the lamb when I brought him home for Elizabeth one Christmas Eve and Elizabeth fed him warm milk from a bottle for a week or more, and he lay on a pillow near her bed.

Everybody loved Worthy very much and put up with the long *baas* which issued from the basement during the winter months before it came time for him to be turned out of doors to gambol in the spring. Inevitably, passers-by took great interest. "Woodrow Wilson kept some on the

White House lawn during the war," an old man told me. "Saved labor."

We gossiped for a while. One advantage about having a sheep is that you get to know your neighbors. Policemen stop too, and one of them paid a call to point out the regulations in a thick book he carried. The regulations forbade "the keeping of livestock," and he and I talked about whether a single lamb constituted "livestock." We decided that maybe it did and maybe it didn't but that Worthy wasn't bothering anybody, and so he went away.

Worthy never did bother anybody except me and maybe Justice Douglas, and the reason was that he refused to think of himself as livestock. As the old man had pointed out, "That one doesn't seem to like grass."

He didn't. He did not go out on the lawn and clip like Woodrow Wilson's sheep but hung around the back door with the dogs, looking for a handout. He ate like the dogs (scraps of lamb, I once noted to my horror). He ran to the fence with the dogs to mark the passing by of other dogs, and most irritatingly, he came into the living room with the dogs whenever someone left the door slightly ajar, so that he could shove it open with his black nose.

It is well-known, I suppose, that unlike a dog, a sheep cannot be housebroken, and Worthy's passing through the living room was always marked. As a veteran cleaner of rugs, I must admit that the marking was relatively easy to repair. Still, like all such markings, it was susceptible to being stepped upon, and then, of course, there was hard work to be done.

For many years, while the children were young, it fell to me to do this work. The younger children were incapable of doing it well, and Joan expressed such horror as to incapacitate her altogether. It occurs to me now that perhaps she wasn't really as horrified as I thought; perhaps I was tricked into showing her that a man was not afraid to get his hands dirty.

As the children grew older, they took over the load; sometimes reluctantly and slowly; sometimes with insufficient application of soda water and salt; always with much argument about which animal was guilty and whose animal that animal was.

With Worthy there was no argument. But neither was there any remedy. In short, Worthy was a mistake, perhaps the worst mistake I have permitted, though not the only one.

I have never been able to figure out what to say to a child who brings home one more dog, or cat, or bird—or, to recall another mistake—one large boa constrictor.

Susan didn't actually bring home the boa constrictor. One night after dinner, there was a knock on the door and two boys, high-school classmates of Susan's, entered, carrying an enormous cage. It was hand-hewn, I could see at a glance, and sturdily constructed, with crossbars and heavy wire screening.

There were white pebbles on the floor of the cage, and the boys spilled a little as they made the sharp turn to get up the stairs to Susan's bedroom. I stooped to pick up the pebbles from the hall rug, and that was when I noticed that inside the cage was an enormous snake, somewhat thicker than my forearm and about eight feet long.

"It's a boa constrictor, for Susan's birthday," said Andy, the most polite as well as the sturdiest of Susan's friends. "It won't bother you any." A lot of work and money had obviously gone into Susan's birthday present. Should I protest?

Anyhow, in this event, Andy turned out to be right—for a while. Ben Boa was a very good and well-behaved snake. Throughout that spring (Susan's birthday is in May) and summer, he lay in his cage, occasionally twining himself around the crossbar and was no bother at all.

I confess that I did not like to see Ben Boa eat. Once a month Susan would ride her bike to a pet store and purchase for a dollar a small white rat, which she would insert into Ben Boa's cage. I saw what happened the very first time and after that I did not watch any more or wish to hear about it from the younger children who not only liked to watch but enjoyed reciting detailed descriptions thereafter.

But aside from eating once a month, which is, after all, a pet snake's due, Ben Boa was no trouble until Mrs. Longworth took an interest in him and after that, he was a great trouble indeed.

Mrs. Longworth heard about Ben Boa at dinner one evening, and it reminded her at once of a pet snake she had kept in the White House, which she had christened Mabel, and which had annoyed her father, President Theodore Roosevelt.

"Only, he couldn't really complain," Mrs. Longworth told the children with that wicked narrowing of the eyes which she adopts when she is describing a victory, "because he had told all the younger ones in the family to love animals and he had given them all permission to bring home a pet.

"So what could Father say when I went out and bought a garter snake?

"But I knew he was awaiting his opportunity. One day when I was sixteen I was invited to a party aboard the Iselin yacht, and I wore Mabel around my neck. Of course, the press got ahold of it and it was in all the papers. Father sent me a telegram: 'Alice, I told you to love animals. I did not tell you to love publicity.'"

When Mrs. Longworth heard about Ben Boa, she insisted at once on seeing him; not only that, but upon having him out of his cage and wrapped around her waist, a procedure which she described as "warming him." The children took up the idea, and from that time, Ben Boa was frequently out of his cage, being warmed.

Particularly of course when Mrs. Longworth came to dinner, and one evening the warming taught me something about the character of Israel's Prime Minister, who was then Ambassador Yitzak Rabin.

Rabin is a short blond man with cold and extremely bright blue eyes and a shy, seemingly diffident manner. He had been a tank commander during the Seven Day War, but he has none of the bluffness which Americans—possibly because of General George Patton—associate with the trade.

He is, however, a man of instant decision, as I learned one evening while we were chatting over a drink in the living room.

Elizabeth entered from another room and rushed up to us wide-eyed. "Dad," she said, "the snake is wrapped four times right around Mrs. Longworth." Elizabeth was excited because four times around was a warming record for Ben Boa. But Yitzak Rabin heard what Elizabeth said and was excited in a different way.

Those blue eyes grew even brighter until they seemed to me to be spitting fire. "A snake around Mrs. Longworth," he repeated quietly, and as he said it his right hand disappeared inside the shoulder of his left sleeve. He had taken two steps toward the other room before I caught him from behind and blurted an explanation.

I caught him in time to prevent myself from learning precisely what he was carrying inside his coat near the left shoulder, but I have a strong suspicion and I rather admired him for being prepared. It wouldn't have done him any good, of course, but he gave the impression of a man who was prepared to fight, with or without weapons and as instantly as occasion might demand.

Inevitably, as Ben Boa was taken out of his cage with greater frequency, somebody would forget to put him back. Customarily on these occasions, it fell to Susan to find him. And one day, she couldn't.

Of all the children in our family, Susan is possessed of the greatest inner calm and fortitude. The disappearance of Ben Boa did not at first distress her. Calmly she hunted the usual places—in drawers, behind doors, on closet shelves, down heating ducts. It was to no avail. Each evening at dinner I asked for the news. Each evening the news was bad. Even Susan began to fret and to conjure in her imagination scenes of vivid doom: Ben Boa out on the sidewalk, accosting a neighbor, wishing perhaps to be "warmed"; the neighbor rushing for a policeman; the policeman drawing a gun.

Such scenes were not beyond the possible, as Mrs. Longworth revealed with practiced malevolence, when she heard that Ben Boa was gone.

"There is," she remarked to a group of women gathered in my living room for some charitable cause to which she herself had summoned them, "an enormous snake loose somewhere in the house." Then turning to three women seated upon the couch, "You know they love to get under the cushions."

I was not present when Mrs. Longworth made this remark but Joan reported that evening that the three women turned pale and that the meeting broke up almost immediately. "It was really over anyhow," she said. "Mrs. Longworth just thought it was time to go."

Joan's recital of the afternoon's events gave us a clue. Susan and Nancy went upstairs and began dumping mattresses on the floor. Under Susan's bed, fully extended in the steel coils, lay Ben Boa, inert and cold.

There is sadness in parting from the familiar even when the familiar is a snake and there was guilt in the knowledge that parting with Ben Boa might have been avoided. Boa constrictors, I discovered by calling the National Zoo, are comfortable at 85 degrees Fahrenheit. Ben Boa's cage contained a light which helped to warm him, though probably not enough. Outside the cage and in the house, he was at seventy degrees, and for a boa constrictor, this is very cold weather. But in this midwinter season, Susan had inadvertently exposed Ben Boa to much worse. Without doubt she stated accurately the cause of death. "Dad, I never should have been sleeping all these nights with the windows open."

It must have been sad for Susan, preparing Ben Boa for burial, getting him out from the bed springs and into a pillow case, but when I came home the following evening she was not at all sad; she was breathless. "Nancy and I dug a hole back of the azalea bushes and we were putting Ben Boa in and the pillow case moved. So we got in the car and drove as fast as we could to the zoo and we went up the wrong driveway and the zoo man stopped us and we explained, and he took Ben Boa and we waited and he came out with the empty pillow case and said he thought Ben Boa would live."

Which Ben Boa did. Indeed, the children visit him once in a while and somewhere in the files

I have an official letter from the zoo thanking me for the donation of one boa constrictor, valued at eighty dollars. Her friend Andy must have liked Susan a lot.

I wish parting with all pets were as happy. It does not seem possible that during a modest lifetime, I have assumed ultimate responsibility for thirteen dogs, five horses, and eighteen cats, as well as the lamb and the boa constrictor.

And I am leaving out birds and a short-lived monkey named Fagin, whose queer, guttural coughing I mistook for monkey chatter when it should have warned me of pneumonia.

They are all gone now—all but four dogs and a single cat—and I believe their souls rest in peace, for without exception they were well treated upon the earth, inoculated, vaccinated, fed, curried and washed, exercised, petted, trained and, where appropriate, housebroken.

And buried. I have been pall bearer at many funerals, and chief consoler to the bereaved. Something about the combination of the words "animal" and "family" foretells certain tragedy, for animals die soon. They die despite care and affection and fences and training. They die under wheels and if not under wheels, they die of old age while children who love them are yet young.

So the child learns tragedy. But he has already learned care and feeding and washing and training and visiting doctors. He has learned hunger and ennui and sheer joy and sickness and recovery. He has learned about growing old. Should he not learn about dying? In the still-mysterious ways by which God governs, isn't this what pets are for?

There was a time before I had children when I owned a large and beautiful German shepherd, and when Thorsten Veblen's famous remark about dogs in his *Theory of the Leisure Class* embarrassed me. "The dog," Veblen wrote, "commends himself to our favor by affording play to our propensity for mastery, and as he is also an item of expense and commonly serves no industrial purpose, he holds a well-assured place in man's regard as a thing of good repute."

Perhaps that is true for old ladies with dachshunds or for single men with German shepherds. But now that I have known all these animals—and dogs in particular—I would rewrite Veblen as follows:

"The dog commends himself to our favor in a way we hesitate to admit, which is that being possessed of an enormous capacity for affection and friendship, and being also short-lived, he exposes our children in the kindest possible way to the sadness and the inevitability of parting."

Castles They Have Known

"A man's house is his castle," said the judge, about halfway through his charge to the jury, and as he cited a nineteenth-century opinion of the California Supreme Court in which the quotation was used, I leaned back in my chair with a tentative sigh of relief.

It was a civil suit, and the amount of money demanded of me was twenty-five thousand dollars, a sum I might have raised, I suppose, if I'd sold most of what I owned.

Moreover, I knew I was guilty of hitting a man. I had hit him square on the mouth with a left hook. "Here," he had shouted, after he sprang into the hallway, and stuck a fistful of papers hard into my chest, "You are served."

Was it wrong to hit him? I wished I hadn't. For here I was in court, and there were the jurors over there in the box, and I didn't know what they were thinking. What do jurors think of a man who hits a process server?

Once more, I went over in my mind the happenings of that morning two years before. It was 6:20 A.M. That had been established in court and I remembered the time vividly because Joan and I were fast asleep when we heard the banging on the door. More important, Elizabeth was asleep and Elizabeth was the one whose sleep we were worried about. Elizabeth was nine at the time and a very sick girl. Whooping cough, or whatever name it is by which doctors might now describe a constant racking which seemed to begin down at the base of her spine and surge upward until her entire body was convulsed. Elizabeth had a pretty small body. Dr. Harvey had come over at midnight and given her something, and about two she went to sleep.

Actually it was Joan who heard the banging first, and she awakened me, tugging at my arm. "Tom, Tom, somebody's at the front door." I had thought it was the middle of the night, but a glance at my wrist watch did not calm me. Whoever it was pounding at the door was pounding hard.

I sprang out of bed and rushed to the stairs. "Just a minute," I said, calling out, and then, more cautiously, "What do you want?"

"Are you Thomas W. Braden?" said the voice outside as I reached the door.

"Yes," I said. "What's the matter?"

"I have a summons for you."

Now, a summons was a fairly ordinary event in my life. I ran a newspaper in Oceanside and

I had about thirty employees, one or more of whom would from time to time run up a bill he couldn't pay, or get in trouble with a finance company. Sometimes, I would be told, via the summons, that I had to garnishee his wages. But the summons was usually delivered by one of the local marshals, and delivered at the office. What was the man doing here at this hour?

I asked him.

In reply, he asked a question too. "Are you going to accept service?"

"No," I said. "You've got a hell of a nerve waking people up at this hour. I've got a sick daughter. Come back at nine o'clock."

At that point, he opened the unlocked door, took a step forward and thrust the summons into my chest.

That was when I hit him. Joan had testified, and the opposing lawyer had drawn from her the admission that when I got out of bed I had been, in her words, "cross." Would that be damaging?

I asked myself honestly whether I had used Elizabeth as an excuse. In part, perhaps. Anger looks for an excuse. Still, the protective instinct is strong at six in the morning when a child is sick and someone is pounding at the door. "A man's home is his castle" seems to me to sum it up accurately.

So I was relieved that the judge included it in the charge to the jury, and included it despite the objection of the other side. It proved, so some of the jurors told me later, to be chief among their considerations in the decision to acquit. I mention it now because it seems to me also chief among the considerations of being a father of eight.

Defensive is how fathers feel about the castles in which they house their children. They would, if they could, build moats and strong walls. But that "something" which Robert Frost described as not liking a wall might be a child. A wall is a challenge to a child and so is a locked front door.

Over and over I explain to my children that it is important to keep the front door locked, and over and over I find it unlocked. It has been a persistent battle between us during our joint occupancy of three castles, none of which I actually ever had to defend, but about all of which I have felt defensive.

One of these was in Virginia, overlooking the Potomac; one in Oceanside, California, overlooking the beach; and one in Maryland, overlooking what David calls "the cultural ghetto" of Chevy Chase. The house in Chevy Chase is bigger than the other houses were, but my guess is that the house in California is the background of their dreams.

The house had been built on the beach in 1929 by a film director named Richard Wallace, and it had been built cheaply, which was lucky for us. For when we moved into it in 1954, there were only three children, and David, the oldest, was four. A house with inner walls made out of thick cardboard is a good house for a family in the process of doubling itself. You rip out the cardboard to enlarge the room or you put in more cardboard to make two rooms.

As the number of people in the family kept changing, the house kept changing. Everybody's room kept changing. "You remember," Nancy now says to Susan, "when we had the bunk beds at the end of the hall in David's room?" And Tommy will say, "David's room wasn't at the end of the hall. David's room was just to the right of the stairs."

And then Nancy will clinch the argument with a line that all except Nicky have been privileged to use: "You don't remember David's old room. You weren't here yet." I don't know whether not having been "here yet" is hard on the psyche. I know that the face of the person who wasn't here yet always falls. It's a hard argument to beat unless you can disprove it, as in, "I was too here yet. I remember the old stairs that led down to the beach outside David's room and Susan had the duck tied by the leg to the bottom stair."

But the one thing that everybody's memory holds in common is the beach. It never changed. Oh, it did change, of course, in the Rachel Carson sense. The tides carried a little away in the winter and brought a little back in July; passing ships jettisoned sludge upon occasion. Once to my horror, a body washed ashore and Joannie and I were down on the beach at the time. It was bloated and bitten, almost unrecognizable as a body, so much so that I didn't have to say it was a body and could hope Joannie wouldn't know. There were stranded porpoises, too, which came ashore, nearly always in the summer, for a reason I don't understand, and the children flocked to watch them, and sometimes a porpoise would recover from whatever ailed him and move on, to accompanying cheers. Each summer, you could see the perch tossing in the green waves. On weekends David fished all day with a long line, and in the evening we ate grilled perch over a beach fire.

We often sang over those fires, lustily and together and without embarrassment, matching our lungs against the timed crash of the waves. The "Battle Hymn of the Republic" became our favorite song, long before Robert Kennedy seized upon it as an unofficial campaign song in 1968. I remember when I first heard the song so used at a Kennedy rally, feeling as though he had taken it away from us. I solaced myself with the contemplation that his children didn't know all four verses.

And each early spring, at midnight or at one in the morning, the grunion ran. "Mom, can I stay up and catch grunion?" It was a happy cry that marked the swing of the seasons and to this day it seems to me much more exciting and zestful and free spirited than "Merry Christmas."

In fact, I look back upon those early years in Oceanside, when I didn't have any money, when the annual payments on the newspaper I had borrowed to buy caused me such worry that sometimes I couldn't sleep, and Joan would wake up and find me sitting on the edge of the bed, just sitting and worrying, and when nobody else in

Oceanside had any money either. So that when I went to collect the bills, the merchant friend would say, "Tom, I don't have any money." I look back on those days and I am grateful to my children because they made me happy nevertheless and "nevertheless," I have always thought, is the only way a human being ever knows what happiness is.

Oh, I had other things to gratify me. One of them was the Oceanside boat harbor on which the mayor and I and Congressman James B. Utt back in Washington worked hard. The Marine Corps had a boat harbor at the very northern edge of Oceanside, but it wasn't any good because it kept filling up with silt, and every few years the Army Corps of Engineers had to spend a hundred thousand or so dredging it out.

I think it was Oceanside Mayor Erwin Sklar's original idea that if the town could get Congress to appropriate a little extra money for the Corps of Engineers, they could dig a boat harbor in Oceanside while they were digging out the old Marine Corps harbor. That would put the town on the map. Why, there wasn't a single boat harbor on the Pacific Coast between San Diego and Newport.

So we all got to work on the idea, and as publisher of the newspaper, I went to meetings and thundered in editorials and wrote letters back to Washington. I think I had some influence too. I know I was mighty proud of that telegram signed John F. Kennedy which came to the office one day. "Happy to inform you that today I signed

H.R. 1362 permitting construction along Ocean-side shore. Congratulations."

Later, I got a pen in the mail—the pen Kennedy used to sign the bill. I had the pen framed, right under the telegram.

Some people in the town complained about our victory. Some of the old-timers said the ocean current running south would hit the jetty and then swirl in and cut the beach away. There's always some opposition to progress. But I was happy, trying to collect bills and being broke and working for a boat harbor and playing with the children.

I learned to surf and the children did, and David worked hard and got good at it, and they all learned to love the sea and to beware of it.

Two events occurred to mar the charm of Oceanside. I'd like to think that both were acts of God and "not my fault," as Nicholas would say. But the first event challenged my duty as a father, and the second came about because I had accepted the duty of being a booster for my town. They accosted me, these two events, like two witches asking questions, and when I had fully committed myself, they struck.

The first event came about as follows: One day, in the summer of 1963, a newcomer appeared on the beach, advertising his presence with a strange device. Workmen came upon the sands and began handling two enormous timbers which, as they were imbedded into place, turned out to be the foundation of a house.

Now, all the beach dwellers of Oceanside lived

along a high bank and descended to the beach by stairways, long stairways—twenty-six at our house (I am a stair counter) and even more at others, depending upon the bank's incline.

And so all the beach houses in Oceanside were protected from the sea, not only in fact but also in style—no picture windows suffering a vista of the sea, but tiny ones with shutters shutting out the sea, the whole imitative of Cape Cod houses, which was sort of silly in a California climate and was not at all atune to modern architecture's attempt to make a house welcome its environment.

But we did have the bunk room, a long, low-ceilinged and narrow hallway which ran the length of the house under the main floor. The bunk room was as close to the sea as you could be and still be in our house and it was, I think, a gay room for guests. Though the opposite of elegant, it had a shower, a couple of tiny dressing rooms, and one bigger room with bunk beds. The only trouble was that to get from the bunk room into the house, you had to go outdoors and walk along the beach side of the house and up a stairway. Guests didn't mind; it gave them privacy. But it bothered me a little, when the family swelled, and Mary, Susan and Nancy had to move down into the bunk room. They were tiny girls, and they were under the roof all right but at night or in the morning, they had to go outside to get in. It bothered me—that bunk room—and it also made me admire the more what I saw rising below and to the right of me upon the sands.

For here was a bunk room better than a bunk room. A bunk room that was also a fully enclosed house. I marveled at the audacity as well as at the skill of modern architecture. Not that this was a mammoth undertaking. It was a small cabin of a house, but the concept upon which it was based was so simple that one wondered, Why didn't I think of that?

"You don't have to build a house high on the bank and descend and ascend stairways all your life," this house seemed to say. "You simply anchor two long beams at the foot of the cliff, sink a couple of cement pillars deep in the sand at the other end of each beam, and there's your foundation. Let the waves roll in under the floor and under the plumbing. They can't hurt anything."

It worked too. Worked exactly. In the highest tides the water almost but not quite touched the floor planks of this new house; and even at low tide, there was enough water so that the front porch not only stared out to sea but was in the sea. A brilliant concept. I made a mental note that one day I should congratulate the owner.

Alas, it was not to be, for when the owner and I met for the first time, it was at one o'clock on a winter's morning, and the mist from the sea rolled in through the windows of the bunk room and I flattened myself against the wall, listened to the footfalls coming up the stairs, listened as the door opened, watched the figure enter the door and stand there, listened to it breathe.

Directly in front of me where I stood at one end of the room, I could see the three little girls in their beds—Nancy at the far end, near where the figure stood; then Susan, then Mary opposite me. To my left, standing at the far end of the room, was Mr. Lorimer.

I had no doubt about it, though in the dark I could not make out his face nor see whether the face wore the horn-rimmed spectacles I had been told to look for. On the previous night all three girls had come flying into the room in their white nightgowns, waking Joan and me with terrified sobs. A man had come into the room, they said, and had stood there and breathed. He had done it before, they were sure. Mary had mentioned it. She had been awake and she had heard footsteps on the stairs, and then heard the door push open, and seen a figure and had been too terrified to cry out. She had not mentioned it to me or to Joan. Maybe it had been a nightmare but now this night she had cautioned her sisters. Nancy had fallen asleep but Susan and Mary had remained awake and they had both heard and seen the figure. "It's Mr. Lorimer, Dad; the man with the new house, and Dad, he just stands there and breathes."

So there I was, the night after that, pressing my body hard against the bunk-room wall. I remained there during what must have been four to five minutes of absolute silence. Outside the waves boomed, and then crashed, and between the boom and the crash, I could hear the clock ticking on the shelf over Mary's bed. Suddenly, the figure at the other end of the room turned, the door opened silently and I heard the footsteps going down the beach stairs.

"Quiet," I whispered loudly to the girls. "Stay right where you are. Don't say a word and don't move." The three little girls were sitting bolt upright in their beds.

Mary whispered, "Dad, was it Mr. Lorimer?"

I did not wait to reply. For when I heard the last footfalls on the wooden stairs, I too went out the door and from the corner of the house, I fixed my eyes upon the patch of beach between the new house and mine. Sure enough, within a minute, the figure of a man walked across that patch of beach, and I followed him with my eyes until they lost him at his back door.

I went back to the bunk room, hugged all the girls and took them upstairs and squeezed them into various beds where sisters and brothers were asleep.

Joan was for calling the police then and there. I decided instead to go see the chief, who was a friend, "in the morning," as I like to say when it's already morning and I haven't been to bed yet.

So that was the way I met Mr. Lorimer. He was, it turned out, a bachelor scion of a rich family who had spent a lifetime living along beaches. My friend, the chief, put a stakeout, consisting of a patrol car, in front of the house on the street and a plainclothesman on the beach side. The plainclothesman picked him up the very next morning on his way up the stairs to the bunk room.

According to the chief, Mr. Lorimer had said, upon being asked to get into the patrol car and answer a few questions, that he had heard that I was away on business a great deal and he worried about whether the little girls were safe. He felt it his duty to go over at night and see.

"Queer duck," said the chief, "but he was scared. I don't think he'll bother you any more."

But Lorimer did bother me. He tabbed me henceforth as an enemy. I heard the neighbors saying that he thought I was dangerously left-wing (Lorimer flew the American flag on top of his new house). Moreover, he met Mary on the beach one day and abused her with such language that a Marine Corps sergeant passing by was made so angry that he went to the county attorney's office and issued a complaint. But these were minor matters. The way Lorimer really bothered me, the way he got me in fact, was that he caused me to remodel the house again.

Out went the bunk room and out came the walls to cover the space where the bunk room had been. And as long as we were doing that, we might as well do this, and about sixty thousand dollars later, there I was with what must still be the most beautiful house along the Oceanside beach.

Beautiful, but purposeless. I had no sooner finished it and begun to pay the new and higher mortgage than the second event struck. It struck slowly, but not so slowly as to be imperceptible.

You could see it coming down the shoreline from the new harbor, moving just a few feet each week, gradual, but final, interesting but awful, natural; therefore remorseless.

Ironic too, I suppose, for I had worked so hard to help build that boat harbor. But it was not the sort of irony at which I could smile. For the beach went when the boat harbor came, just as the anti-progress old-timers had predicted that it would. First, the currents hit the new jetty and swerved around it and began to scoop the beach. Then the currents brought in all the rock which the engineers had removed for the boat harbor. They piled the rock high along the shore; at first on the jetty's protected side, then foot by foot and yard by yard, along the beach to my new house and beyond.

It's sad to see that house now. It sits there high on the bank, the great glass window looking out from where the bunk room used to be; looking toward the ocean where the beach and the touch football and the bonfires used to be; looking out on a hundred yards and more of piled-up rock.

You'd have to wear heavy shoes and dungarees now to reach the ocean from the house, and you'd have to be prepared to climb hills of rock. When you had scrambled over all the rock, you would not be able to swim because the current is still dragging large boulders to pile up against large boulders, and each wave can kill.

The money I spent on the house is gone along with the beach. Who wants to buy a beach house that has become a rock house?

As I say, it's sad to see it, and I did go back and look at it just the other day. An expensive derelict, that house. There was only one consolation. Standing there on the rocks with Dr. Harvey, viewing the desolated scene, it occurred to me to ask myself how Mr. Lorimer had survived progress. And I looked over at Lorimer's house. You know what? There were piles of rock where Mr. Lorimer's house had been, but Mr. Lorimer's house was gone.

Dad Shouts Too Much

On the beach at Oceanside we built great bonfires and sang into the night about railroads and
silver dollars and being "five hundred miles from
home." The waves broke heavily on the flat, wet
sand below our fire, and the pounding rever-
berated, so that you had to sing very loud to
encourage a child to sing too.

With all her many attributes, Joan has a single
fault: She cannot carry a tune. So it was up to
me to set an example for shy children, and it
may be that those fourteen years of beach sing-
ing account for my tendency to stentoriousness.

Or it may be that having been trained early in
life as a platoon leader, and finding myself now
with half a platoon, it seems natural to bark out
orders in an extremely loud voice so as to be
heard above the sound of jeeps and half tracks
and Nicholas saying: "I'm nine years old and I'll
do what I want to do."

Anyhow, Joan says I am loud and all the children have echoed her criticism, so that when in bantering conversation at dinner, we list each other's faults, it is agreed by all that "Dad shouts too much."

I feel correctly chastened. I envy the quiet and the calm. Are there fathers who can accomplish order or a warning with a nod or a raised eyebrow? Surely there are times when there is nothing to do except shout.

I remember once in the army in Italy making a terrible mistake which only a strong voice could correct. We had to cross a shallow river, and to get to the crossing point, we were to follow a narrow muddy road along the bank and then make a sharp right-hand turn at a junction. The turn was important, I explained to the four truck drivers as we halted under a tree and looked at the map under a flashlight, because anyone who continued straight on would sooner or later hit the German lines.

And so we set out and I was first in the jeep and the trucks carried the guns behind. It was very dark and we were driving without lights, so we drove very slowly. Maybe that was why when I reached the turn, it did not occur to me to drop off a man as a guide. Of course, I should have done that. Any fool would have done that. But I could see the truck behind me; its driver could see me making the turn. There was a truck right behind him. Anyhow, I didn't set a man out as a guide.

Up the road a little bit after the turn, I stopped

and looked back. I could see three trucks following me. But I couldn't see four. I got out of the jeep and I began to run, and as I ran, past one and then two and then three trucks, panic struck me, and I ran harder and faster and as I ran I shouted as long and as hard as I could shout.

"Stein! Stein! Stein! Turn back, Stein!" I wonder if the Germans heard it, splitting the damp night air and coming back at me from the thickness of the woods along the road. It was a good name to shout at Germans, and Stein, the driver of the fourth truck, must have had good ears to hear the distant shout above the slow grinding of his gears.

Stein stopped. He said later that he was having qualms at not seeing anything ahead and that he might have stopped anyhow. But the fact is he heard me and if he and the other members of his gun crew are still alive today, they owe it to the luck that their stupid platoon leader possessed at least the ability to shout.

I've thought about that river crossing often because it seems to me that whereas some men live lives through stages, as in Shakespeare, my life has been arrested and I am doomed to the perpetual task of getting people across a river, shouting as I go.

We were hiking once in Colorado and I looked back up the mountain path down which we had come and saw Joannie, aged eight, sitting on a ledge overlooking a drop of some two hundred feet. She had wandered off the path and slid down a very steep bank of granular rock. Looking over the outcrop, she was terrified, unable to get back up. She sat there, clutching onto herself, and as I later learned, crying out, "Dad, Dad," though I could not hear her.

It seemed to me, looking up at the tiny figure against the sky, that she was in the grip of vertigo and that if she stood, she might become dizzy and fall. I shouted to her, so loudly that I aroused the curiosity of a Basque shepherd from a nearby meadow and he came galloping up on horseback and reached Joannie before me.

I still carry, in my mind's eye, the picture of that rough and bearded man, looking like some wild Tartar, plunging his horse down onto the ledge, and swooping Joannie up in front of him, grasping her easily with one arm. It is a good picture to carry around in the head, except that it makes me something of a fool. I say to myself, "Well, at least I shouted. Otherwise, he would not have come."

What bothers me about the criticism of my family is not that I shout too much but what I shout. What I shout is so devoid of intellectual content, so unworthy of the life I have lived and of the wisdom which books and teachers and good friends have tried to impart. The things I shout make trivial and silly the notion that between generation and generation the torch is passed.

"Turn off the water!" "Put down that lighter fluid!" "Look behind before you cast that fly rod." "Wait! Don't dive!" "Hey! Come back here! You haven't made your bed."

Is this the kind of wisdom Longfellow imparted to his grandchildren between romps during the children's hour? Is this what Winston Churchill thought was missing from the education of the "untutored striplings" to whom he hesitated to pass the lamp?

How sad that three-quarters to four-fifths of that which a father imparts to his children should consist of such commonplace warnings that it is almost embarrassing to put them in writing.

And yet if I were asked to name the attributes essential to a father of eight, I should unhesitatingly place among the chief, the ability to shout for attention, not only over distance but over rivals, whether animate or no. My shouts, I firmly believe, have saved eyes, and prevented broken necks, burns and death by automobile. They have summoned help and brought home stragglers. They have overridden argument at times when argument meant delay and when delay meant danger. Also, they have summoned the guilty to justice when the guilty were about to flee.

I justify this last as a contribution to family discipline and therefore to the general welfare but I would agree that the contribution is made at some cost to immediate peace of mind. Joan says that the shout disturbs almost as much as the cluttered-up room or the unmade bed which provokes it.

But when a father is standing in the middle of the cluttered-up room looking at the unmade bed and sees out the window the child halfway down the street and moving fast, he must make an immediate choice. Rightly or wrongly, my choice is to shout.

I suppose that a father of one child might choose to wait until the child came home from the friend's house or the baseball game and then speak to him quietly about duty undone. But more than three children mitigate against this course. With eight, a man would have to keep a reminder list. For with eight, it is certain that something else will turn up that will call for shouting. In a family of eight children that child who is not immediately chided may never be chided and his escape is unfair to him who is caught red-handed.

For many years I told myself that the time would come when the family would live without much shouting, that as the children grew older, the need for warning would fade and so would the shout of outrage at discovery of neglect. I had forgotten about the telephone.

As the children grow older, the telephone becomes more and more important to their daily lives, so that after school and when they are all home at Christmas time and during the summer, the house rings with shouting.

There is no other way. A buzzer system is a waste of money. No child is ever in his room when he is wanted on the telephone. He is out in the yard playing touch football or he is in some other child's room or he is in the kitchen getting something out of the refrigerator, or he is not there at all but has gone down the street to visit a neighbor, a fact which is only revealed by his not answering his shouted name.

I have tried a separate number and a separate listing—"Braden children." The telephone company suggested this and it did save Joan and me from shouting for a few days, until the children's friends learned that when "Braden children" was busy, "Braden" would do as well.

Our friends, too, when they could not get us, rang on the children's line. Joan was on our phone telling a reporter from the New York *Post* that she hadn't talked to Henry Kissinger for months and therefore had no knowledge of his state of mind or whether he intended to remain at his post or resign (he was then a White House assistant). When Tommy burst into the bedroom shouting at the top of his lungs, "Mom, Henry Kissinger is on the other line. He says, 'What time is dinner?,'" the reporter was cool. "Go ahead and take it," she told Joan. "I'll call you back in ten minutes."

So we have become a family of shouters. I shout in warning or reprobation and they shout in summons, and only when we are together assembled at meals is one of us not shouting at or for another.

As a result, the children have become extremely quiet when they are away from home. I am told by Susan's friends at college and by Joannie's and Mary's that they speak in virtual whispers, and David, who has survived the shouting longer than the rest, has become so silent that his friends wonder whether he is fulfilling a vow.

It is, I am sure, a kind of protest against shouting and against me. I'd like to join it. There will come a time, I hope, when the children, grown to full estate, will remark to their children or to future wives and husbands not yet known, that "Dad [meaning me] never raises his voice these days." I hope so. I want it to be that way. But as I look back upon the bonfires and the swimming pools and the hikes, and as I mentally tote up the number of telephone calls, the answering of which has fallen by chance to me, I think I shall know—even if they do not—that one of the reasons they all survived and grew up and got married and had children of their own, was that Dad had a strong pair of lungs.

Mother's Rule

Every summer since David was old enough to read, I have prepared children's book lists for vacation reading. On the whole, the effort has not been successful, and I find myself doing it today out of habit and hope rather than confidence. Some of the books get read by some of the children, but the fact of an official list turns what might be fun into avoidable duty.

A better idea, it seems to me, is to go out and buy a lot of books—all the classic children's books—and put them on the shelf and say nothing about it. Don't say they are on the shelf or brag about what you have done. Say nothing.

Then later on—a year or so later on—you give Tommy a job, like mowing the lawn, and he says he can't do it alone and you say, "Tom Sawyer knew how to get a fence whitewashed." You can tell from Tommy's eyes that he knows that story.

Or Elizabeth, far too young to drive a car, says

she wants to drive a car. You say, "You remember what happened to Toad in *The Wind and the Willows?*" Elizabeth laughs and you know that Elizabeth knows. You may gloat.

But if there is some book you feel a child must read, a book you consider absolutely essential to his learning and upbringing, you must follow my mother's rule.

"All classics and 'good' books were ruined for me," my mother wrote at the age of seventy-seven. "To this day I have to force myself even to read anything *about* a book like *War and Peace.* The 'good' books we force upon the young in contravention of our knowledge that the purpose of the young is to contravene. Therefore, learning must be secret and illegal. If you really want a child to read something, there is only one way: Hide it."

My mother insisted that nobody had ever tried her rule. But I have. It works. I hide the "good" books, or I put them on the highest shelves. "These books up there are very personal," I say, as I do so, "I wish you wouldn't touch them." It is a sure way to get a child to read anything you want him to read, from the *Iliad* to the Bible.

The opposite works too. Are there any books you do not want the children to read? Do you have any "dirty" books? *Lady Chatterley's Lover? Justine? Memoirs of Hecate County?* Do not put them on a high shelf or in an out-of-the-way place, or warn any child not to read them. If you do, they will.

Mother's rule works for other things than books.

It worked, for example, in the case of the visit of Mollie Parnis, the New York dress designer, whose kindness to my daughters embarrassed me greatly until I thought to apply mother's rule.

Mollie Parnis came to spend a weekend with us on a recent spring, and this in itself was mildly disconcerting because, as one of the world's most accomplished and successful dress designers, Miss Parnis has long been able to accustom herself to comforts I cannot provide.

But she is such a genuinely friendly and warm person that I might have been able to put out of my head such worries as how she was going to get along in the spare bedroom with dogs and cats walking in and out most of the night, and a baseball game likely to start outside her window at 7 A.M. on the Saturday morning of her rest had it not been for the gifts she brought when she came.

Mollie arrived in an airport-rented limousine, explaining that she had to have a chauffeur bring her "because of the boxes." The boxes were dresses; one for each of my daughters, five in all, and they made an imposing stack on the hall rug, once the chauffeur had set them down.

Opened, in the living room thereafter, they made me nervous. They were beautiful dresses. Some were simple, long, sleek and clinging; some were short and gay with pink ribbons and a certain swash. I knew, moreover, that they were expensive dresses. Three hundred dollars each? Five hundred? Naturally, I didn't ask. The moment was coming, I knew, when the price of the dresses would cross Mollie's mind.

For, of course, there was no way to get out of it. The girls must come down and try them on. Mollie had estimated sizes carefully, but as they trooped into the living room in their bib overalls and boots, and I heard her say, "It doesn't really matter; if someone likes someone else's, they can be altered, you know," my heart sank.

For there they were, standing there, all five of them, as I say, in their bib overalls and boots, dressed as though for going fishing, but also—I knew and I knew Mollie did not—they were dressed as they wanted to be dressed, and as they thought it right and proper to dress.

I must say in their behalf they were good about it. They emitted minor exclamations as they opened the boxes, and they did actually take out the dresses and hold them up and most of them tried one on for size. I thought they looked great in their dresses. All of a sudden they had legs—quite good legs—and breasts—quite good breasts.

But they didn't think they looked great and you could see they didn't. By the time it was time for trying on the other dress, or time for Mollie to suggest more specifically the minor alteration she had noted, they had all sort of drifted off, and Joan and Mollie and I sat before the piles of paper and the half-empty boxes and the dresses draped on chairs, and felt suddenly alone.

I was profuse in my thanks and so was Joan. For that matter, the girls had all said "Thank you." But somehow, I knew that Mollie knew, and I knew she must have been disappointed. We had a good weekend. Tommy did not get up a baseball game outside Mollie's window and the girls all went off to swim at a quarry they know about in Virginia and were home in time for dinner and were pleasant at the table. But nothing more was said about the dresses.

Until after Mollie left. And then I asked Nancy, who happened to be there, and I asked in an understanding way. I asked, "Can't you girls wear any of those dresses Miss Parnis brought for you?" And Nancy looked at me, a look that said "This is very secret," and then she wrinkled her eyebrows. So I knew.

And then as if to spare my feelings, Nancy said, "Some people might, Dad. You know, the kind of people whose mothers dress them up or something. But it *was* nice of her."

And so the Mollie Parnis dresses were put away, upstairs in the attic, in what we call the enormous room, a room full of Joan's old clothes and shoes, by far the most expensively furnished room in the house. And I tried, with some success, to put the failure out of mind.

Until one day, just this past summer, when it occurred to me to try out Mother's rule.

As I think I have made clear, all my daughters wear either blue jeans or bib overalls or old pairs of pants, and wear them at all times. I think I have not mentioned the exception. They wear them at all times, except when you would expect them to wear them, such as to a barn dance.

For a barn dance, they go to their mother's

closet in the bedroom and take her most expensive dresses, showing a preference for those which have been newly cleaned and are wrapped in cellophane for the next occasion on which Joan wishes to wear them.

Partly because she works hard all day at an office, Joan is never quite ready to go out to dinner when the hour comes. I stand downstairs and say, at first calmly and then, as five-minute intervals elapse on my watch, with increasing annoyance, "Joan, are you coming?" And she calls back, "Yes, I am coming. Just a minute." But sometimes she varies this routine. Sometimes she appears in person at the top of the stairs, without her dress on and she says, "Do you know what they did? I had my good white dress cleaned and ready and I just put it on and and it has a spot and a dirty neck." And then she adds, "It makes me so cross I can't stand it."

Joan never swears, never takes the name of the Lord in vain; very seldom gets angry, always understates her own emotions. But when she says she is "cross" she means she is about to go up the wall, and she is almost never "cross" except when one of the girls steals a dress.

One day last summer when Joan was out of town, I heard about the barn dance. I heard it from Susan, who said her friend, Mary Adams, was giving a barn dance and they were all going— Susan, Nancy, Joannie, Mary, even Elizabeth. Nothing was said about clothes, but I knew.

I also knew there was nothing I could do to prevent it. If I said, "I hope you won't take your mother's clothes," they would tell me that Joan had said they could; or that they were going to wear one of the old dresses put away in the enormous room. But something would go awry with that plan. The old dress would not fit, or would have "a big tear," and this having been discovered at the last minute, there would be really nothing to do but to go to the bedroom and get one of the new ones.

I had been through this before. I knew what would happen. And then I bethought myself of the Mollie Parnis dresses. I wondered if I could find them.

It was very hot in the enormous room, and the dresses hung thick and close together, separated once in a while by some little boy's suit that Tommy or Nicholas or David had worn once or twice or perhaps not at all.

But I found what I thought were the Mollie Parnis dresses, or at least some of them, and I took some downstairs the morning after I had talked to Susan and hung them in Joan's closet—not all together, but interspersed among Joan's clothes.

I was not there when the girls left for the barn dance, and I had been long asleep when they returned. But two adults whom I saw later in the week described my daughters as "knockouts," and Joannie said to me on the next morning, which was Sunday, "Dad, four people told me I was beautiful."

I said, "Congratulations. What dress did you wear?"

"Mother's," Joannie answered.

"Which one?" I asked in casual disapproval, and I looked up from the newspaper I was reading in bed. "Show me."

Joan's closet is right across from the bed, and it was open, and all her dresses were visible. So I did not have to strain to see the dress to which Joannie pointed. "Pretty, isn't it?" she asked.

"Yes," I said. "Very pretty, but you shouldn't have worn it." I could hardly wait until she left the room to get out of bed and go look at the label. Mother's rule had worked again.

One must not push Mother's rule to the point of expecting that everything the rule entices a child to read will be something the child will like. I think, for example, of *A Treasury of the Familiar*, a book I like because it contains much of what I'd read as a boy, none of which my children read now.

Not that "Paul Revere's Ride" is great poetry, nor "Old Ironsides" nor "The Last Leaf." Nor that Webster wasn't florid nor Tennyson imperialist nor Longfellow sentimental.

But it does seem to me that children ought to know some of these speeches and poems which their fathers, grandfathers, and great-grandfathers knew by heart; not necessarily to like them, but to know they exist. Is it sentimental of me to think that children might want to know? My children ask me, "Dad, who was Oliver Wendell Holmes?" or "Who was Ralph Greenleaf Whittier?" They have run across the names in some social history of the United States. They have read

Yeats, Frost, Stevens. But they have never read Longfellow, Bryant, Coleridge or Wordsworth.

My friend Stewart Alsop gave me *A Treasury of the Familiar* not long before he died, and I used it as bedside reading for a number of weeks. Having concluded that it contained things the children ought to read, I put it, when I had finished, on the highest shelf in the back bedroom—a shelf too high for me to reach without a stepladder. It was the same shelf and in the same spot where I had once attempted to hide De Sade's *Justine*, a book I later found at David's bedside. Joannie was the first to bite on *A Treasury of the Familiar*. I found her looking through it one evening while she was listening to records and I was preparing for bed.

"Oh," I said, feigning surprise, "that's the book Stewart Alsop gave me."

"Yes," said Joannie, "there's an awful lot of bullshit in it. Listen to this: 'The mossy marbles rest/On the lips that he has pressed/In their bloom.'"

I was a trifle saddened. Maybe she's right. Maybe, I reflected, everything I ever thought romantic when I was young was bullshit. But I was not altogether downhearted. At least Joannie would not again ask, "Dad, who was Oliver Wendell Holmes?"

Our Rules

There are rules for living with eight children which I have found to stand the test of time.

Rule One: Nobody can go to the bathroom. I speak, of course, of trips in the car across the country or on weekend drives of length and duration. I speak also of the dinner table, and in particular of the dinner table at a public restaurant. A child of between five and ten who insists on having to leave the table in order to go to the bathroom is probably bored, and this may be my fault. It is at least worth the effort of trying to engage him in conversation and it is surprising, once this is accomplished, how often he quickly forgets that he wanted to go to the bathroom.

A child between ten and, say, fifteen who insists upon going to the bathroom from the dinner table usually goes in order to smoke a cigarette. Below the age of sixteen in our family it is forbidden to smoke. I don't say the injunction has always been obeyed. But it still stands.

Obviously the bathroom rules cannot be enforced to the point of cruelty or embarrassment, but if the rule is mentioned frequently enough during the early years, it takes hold and need seldom be mentioned again.

Rule Two: Everybody eats the same thing. At home, of course, this rule merely states reality. It is abroad that it is necessary. Try going into a Howard Johnson's sometime with eight children, each of whom wants a different main course and none of whom can quite make up his mind about dessert or "beverage," as waitresses in Howard Johnson's say.

I invented the rule at a Howard Johnson's during a trip across the country. It was early evening. We had a little farther to go, and so, perhaps, did everyone else who had stopped at Howard Johnson's. The place was packed, the waitresses overbusy, and everyone seemingly in a hurry.

The menu was, as usual, full of choices, and a children's menu made choice more complicated. Eight different main courses had been ordered and six different flavors of ice cream and Tommy had decided to switch his order from the children's menu to the adult because on the children's menu you only got vanilla ice cream. Through all, I forbore and thought it was at last over and then, as an afterthought, the waitress said, "And what kind of dressing would you like on your salad? Roquefort, French, Thousand Island or Italian?" And Susan said, "What's in Italian?" and I made up the rule.

From that time on, we enter the restaurant, we sit down, we look at the menu and we have a short discussion. I assess the various points of view and then the rule comes into play: Everyone eats the same thing and I'm the one who says to the waitress, "We'll have ten."

Rule Three: Lay Not Up Treasures. This is a rule I dislike a lot and I wish I did not have to hold to it. But over the years I have found too many of my children in tears or rages about the loss of their treasures to their brothers and sisters to come to any other conclusion than that with eight children, property cannot be hoarded.

This is not to say that there can be no property: Tommy's bicycle is Tommy's and does not belong to Nicholas. Susan's dress is Susan's, not Joannie's. But it is Tommy's bicycle or Susan's dress only so long as it is in use by its owner, can be defended by its owner, or complained about if borrowed. What we have learned over the years is that we cannot hoard or store or put away.

As the oldest, David has suffered most from this rule, and suffered before it was a rule. I was as outraged as he when he discovered, after six months' absence in Venezuela, that the possessions he had put away in his room had been rifled, his books dispersed, his pocket knife gone, his baseball glove and the football which was "Official NFL." I made a scene about it. I said, "Can't anybody in this house put something away and expect to find it when he gets back?"

The answer to that question is "Not if he has seven brothers and sisters." As further experience buttressed the answer, it was necessary to prevent future shock by laying down the rule.

I don't know whether I ought to be embarrassed about this, or whether it is a tribute to pragmatism. The children do not think of themselves as stealing from one another. If Susan's bicycle is down in the basement and she is away and will be away and cannot use her bicycle, why can't Nancy ride it?

Maybe another way of stating the rule is that in a large family, all property is tainted by commonality. Things are to be used. If your brother or sister is not using a thing, use it.

Rule Four: Your Turn Next. Joan and I say those words a lot, often in response to the question: "When do I get to go?" But it works in many other situations too. It is strictly enforced because it is self-enforcing, both ways. I can't buy four or five bicycles at Christmas, so I buy one. "It's your turn next," I say to him or her who doesn't get a bicycle, and there is no doubt that I shall be reminded.

Rule Five: Let's Let Nicholas Talk. It used to be Tommy and then Elizabeth and then Susan and so on up the line. The youngest in a large family has a difficult time getting to say anything because other voices are larger and more authoritative.

But not necessarily more conducive to the enjoyment of a meal. Nancy said one night at dinner that in the event Nelson Rockefeller ever ran for

President, he would lose because of his record as Governor of New York. "Attica?" I ventured, referring to the controversy still going on about Rockefeller's conduct of the prison riot. "No," said Nancy, "I mean the laws he put through about penalties for possession of drugs. They're horrible, and they haven't done any good."

This provoked vigorous discussion around the table and when it had subsided a little, I asked Nancy why, even supposing that the Rockefeller laws were as bad as she said, they would cause him to lose an election.

"Because all young people will vote against him," she answered. Right away the discussion became generational, Joan and I maintaining that the average voter was middle-aged; Nancy holding that the near unanimous desire on the part of the eighteen- to twenty-one-year-olds for retribution against Rockefeller—that and the righteousness of their cause—would carry the day. It was an argument that got nowhere. Nancy was growing angry. The other children were taking her side. We were facing the kind of blow-up which is not uncommon at our dinner table.

And so I said, "Let's let Nicholas talk." And everybody fell silent and Nicholas gulped and said, "Well," and brushed his hair back out of his eyes and told us about how the Egyptians buried their kings. He described the tunnels inside the pyramids and the routes of the grave robbers who wound their way to treasure nonetheless, and wound up with a dazzling description of the treasure which the robbers found.

Nicholas had learned about the Egyptian kings that day in school and I found his story fascinating and infinitely peaceful, and now whenever there is an argument at dinner which threatens to test our tempers or to send someone rushing from the table in tears, I say, "Let's let Nicholas talk."

Rule Six: Take an Aspirin and Lie Down. This rule has been enforced in our family for some twenty years, and it is really Joan's rule. "Take an aspirin and lie down" is her remedy for every illness, and she is proud of the fact that through eight children, she has yet to purchase a thermometer.

And never really needed one. The only time anybody in the family was thermometer-sick, she really wasn't. I mean, we all thought little Joannie had had appendicitis. We thought so for many years. And then one day, I was playing golf with Dr. Harvey and we reached the eighth tee of the Oceanside golf course. It is a far-off tee, placed against the stubble of unused fields, and so it is a good tee for confidences.

Stub and I had been talking casually about his job as a doctor as compared to mine as a newspaper editor, and I asked him whether he had ever made any ghastly mistakes.

"Not really ghastly," he answered, and then squinted at me sideways and pursed his lips the way Stub does when he is about to tell a plain truth. "I've made a few small mistakes," he said, "like Joannie's appendix."

I remembered the night of Joannie's appendectomy. It was one of the occasions when Joan's rule had seemed harsh and unmotherly. Joannie had been awake half the night with a pain she was too young to locate precisely or to explain and Stub had come and probed with his fingers and tried to establish by this procedure whether the sincerity of Joannie's cry proved the location of the pain. And at last he made the diagnosis: To the hospital at once.

"I made a nice incision," he said, "and there was the appendix and I looked across the table at John [his partner] and he looked at me and we just rolled our eyes. It was as healthy an appendix as anybody ever saw."

So they took it out and little Joannie never will have appendicitis. But the point is she never did. The rule still stands. You're not really sick. Take an aspirin and lie down.

The Non-Conformists

At the beginning, there was David, who spent
most of his childhood holding a short pole with
a string tied to one end and pretending to fish,
under the dining room table, or the piano or whatever roof he could find.

David grew up to be a very private person,
wearing his privacy in public as Mr. Nixon's men
wore their patriotism. The red hair grew very
long—down to the shoulders and then beyond the
shoulders, and became a badge of privacy that
seemed to me to flaunt privacy in the same way
that the little American flags in the buttonholes
of Mr. Nixon's men seemed to me to flaunt patriotism. But I have never been able to persuade
David that his hair is anomaly to his purpose
and that it makes some people angry and frightened.

Like the policeman who stops him on the highway for tossing a cigarette out of the window;

or like the sheriff in Freeburg, Missouri, who greeted him coming out of a restaurant: "My job, boy, is to escort you to the town line. Here in Freeburg we don't tolerate folks like you." He may have been surprised to find that the boy with the too-long red hair had a valid driver's license, and nothing in his pockets to warrant an arrest, but the hair made up his mind. He escorted him. There was a time when David might have had something in his pockets to warrant an arrest. But that is another story and belongs under the chapter heading "The Anti-Saloon League and Me." David no longer carries marijuana.

He is quick; he is bright; he is an expert fly fisherman, a good soccer player and skier, a painter, a poet, a lumberjack and a construction worker. He has read all the books my mother told me to read—from Shakespeare to Ben Jonson, from Voltaire to Molière. He has traveled to Crete and to Afghanistan and to Venezuela. He speaks fluent French and Spanish. But David has no formal education. He will not go to college.

He laughs at me in my gray suit and striped tie and ironed shirt. I should like to get him to conform too, but whenever I think about it, there comes before my mind's eye a picture of myself and him which makes me ashamed.

We are on a beach and we are playing touch football; my team against Dr. Harvey's team. Up above us on the cliff to the left is our house, a gray dormitory of sea-sprayed wood with many windows. To our right is the sea, and the waves crash evenly and loudly. When they tumble, one has to shout so that the team members can hear the signals. These touch football games began as family affairs with Joan and little children—Dr. Harvey's and mine—participating, and neighborhood kids who would drop over every Sunday afternoon to play.

But they got out of hand; they got serious and big and the idea was to win. Active recruiting took place from around the town and from nearby Camp Pendleton. One winter, the participants included Princeton's tail back of two seasons previous, an end from Bowdoin and a quarterback from Seton Hall. But Dr. Harvey and I continued as regulars, and so, by virtue of his relationship to me rather than his size and age, did thirteen-year-old David.

I have forgotten what the score was—nothing to nothing, I suspect—but I remember that I had cut out left, and I turned to watch the ball arching high. It was a long pass, thrown by the Princeton tail back, and it floated to the corner near a large pile of sharp rocks which marked the imaginary goal line. There was David, racing in the clear, arms outstretched, reaching as the ball came down, taking it. And then, unbelievably, he dropped it. "God," I said, "you didn't—you didn't drop it!" The exclamation is one I have taken back a thousand times in the years that have passed. Was the long hair, the "that's your bag, Dad," the iconoclast who was to come—was that a fear of failure, a desire to stand aside, and was that my fault?

Maybe it would have happened anyhow, by

nature or by the fashioning of the times. Maybe I blame myself too much. But I have to blame myself for the one result I know was a result, which was that David never played in those Sunday afternoon football games again.

I worry about the radicalization of my daughter Mary. She went off to the University of California at Santa Barbara, a sweet, trusting, pretty blond girl with sloe eyes; graceful, and retaining from childhood a distinctive and rather attractive habit of walking upon her tiptoes, as though she were entering a room where good friends were asleep.

She came back from the University of California at Santa Barbara wearing clod hoppers and blue jeans, hard-eyed, loud-voiced, old-shirted, and above all, angry. Angry, I noticed first, at Henry Kissinger. Casually, on the evening that she arrived home from college for her first vacation, her mother mentioned that Henry Kissinger was coming to dinner.

Mary's voice was full of scorn and her lips over-actuated, a habit I have since noted, common to people her age who try to make up in exaggeration of expression what they are not sure about in fact. "You're having a murderer to dinner, Mom? Henry Kissinger likes to kill babies."

Joan was shocked. She and Henry Kissinger have been friends for a long time, ever since one of the presidential campaigns of Nelson Rockefeller, for whom they both worked hard. "Henry Kissinger is a friend," Joan said to Mary, maintaining calm. "He is my friend. I expect you to behave as I would behave toward a friend you had invited to dinner."

"One thing I will never do, Mom," Mary answered, "is invite a murderer to dinner."

That was during her freshman year. Subsequently, there was a riot at the University of California at Santa Barbara, during which the Bank of America was burned down. As I recall, it was burned down twice. The bank rebuilt its building and the students accepted the challenge and burned it down again. At any rate, the next time I saw Mary I inquired about the bank. "Did you see it happen?" I asked in the sympathetic tone with which one addresses an innocent young person who by accident of circumstance has been forced to witness crime. "Of course," said Mary, "I was standing across the street demonstrating." "My God," I gasped, "you didn't have anything to do with it, did you?" "Well," she said, "I didn't plant the bomb. I'm not even sure I approve of it. If you think of it as a bank, why the bank wasn't really hurting anybody. But if you think of the bank as representing the system, then, of course . . ." She shrugged.

I was thunderstruck. With difficulty, I refrained from starting my rejoinder with the phrase "No daughter of mine . . ." So I said, instead, "Burning a building is a crime. Burning this building was a mob crime, which is the most dangerous because the most contagious of crimes." Something like that. I remember that I spoke slowly and chose my words with care. But I shall remember Mary's rejoinder through the years to come. "I can see," she said, "how, according to your understanding of society, you would think so."

I said nothing. What was I supposed to say? Or do? You can't spank a nineteen-year-old. Besides, spanking Mary would provide her with precisely the evidence of brutal oppression which she seeks. Take her out of college? Education. A college education, so I was taught to believe, next to earning a living, was life's major goal.

Then what? It all seemed so sad. There she was once, I reflected, a nice little girl, getting good grades behind the protective stone walls of the Bishop's School. And here she is now, still getting good grades . . . wait a minute. Hadn't I read that there were professors and instructors at the University of California at Santa Barbara who were also charging the bank and demonstrating in the streets? Good grades. You don't get good grades if your professors and instructors are displeased. Was my daughter no rebel after all? Was she perhaps a conformist?

I looked at her again and I thought I saw her as she really was, repeating the political views of the recent Ph.D.'s who were her instructors, many of whom, as Henry Kissinger remarked in conversation, suffered from "occupational guilt" because earning their Ph.D.'s had permitted them to avoid the draft. She was dressed in the baggy blue jeans, the old shirt, the clod hoppers. She was wearing the regulation uniform and thinking the regulation thought. Suddenly, it all seemed clear. Mary was conforming, as I had once conformed, indeed as in my gray suit, my black shoes, my striped tie, I conformed now. "The thing to do with Mary," I said to myself, "is wait." So I am waiting.

Facing the New Morality

Lewis Mumford, the historian-critic, told me when I was in college that through thirteen centuries the ethical code of mankind had not changed. I was too unwitting—or maybe too shy—to ask him whether he included abstention from fornication in the ethical code of mankind, but I presume he did. The major ethical works that I now know about prohibit it, and the Bible, for example, waxes extremely wroth on the subject, particularly in the Book of Revelations.

But the ethical code of mankind must have changed sometime after I left college and before my daughter entered. I can't place the year; I can only say that the change came to my attention in the fall of 1973, during a conversation with a dean at Antioch College in Yellow Springs, Ohio.

It was not a satisfactory conversation. "My daughter," I said to the dean, "is a freshman student at your college and two things happened to her recently which upset her very much. First, she studied late at your college library the other evening, and arriving at her room, she discovered that her roommate was in bed with . . . yes, that's right. And the bed was only a foot away from her bed, and it was embarrassing, you see, and so she has a problem here that I don't think she ought to have.

"And then, second, she went off to a meeting last Tuesday of one of the clubs on your campus. She arrived a trifle late and opened the door to find a darkened room with a naked girl stretched out on the table while the other girls were sort of probing her and taking flash pictures at close range. 'Get to Know Your Body' was the theme of the meeting. My daughter was upset. In fact, she burst into tears while she was telling me about it."

I told the dean that I didn't want Joannie, who was seventeen, to know I had called him and I said I wasn't exactly complaining but only reporting and asking for information. "What is the policy of Antioch," I asked, "on the subject of morality?" The dean did not answer my question then and there but said he would like a little time to look into the matters I had reported and that he would then get back to me.

When I hung up the telephone, I was worried. Would my call embarrass Joannie? Would deans come poking around asking questions of her roommate and banning a campus club? Would Joannie be branded as a prude or a stool pigeon?

I needn't have worried. The dean didn't ask any questions that Joannie was made aware of, either embarrassingly or, for that matter, at all. And he never called me back. I think he thought I was the prude and the stool pigeon, though it was about that time that Antioch's Yellow Springs campus erupted in a student strike which closed the campus down and it may be that the dean simply had other things to do.

Moreover, I do not intend to single out Antioch as possessed of more sin than other campuses. Now that fornication can be accomplished with little or no possibility that children will ensue, the words of the Jew of Malta strike a humorous note. "Thou hast committed fornication" is not much more guilt inspiring than "Look not upon the wine when it is red." Because morals tend to bolster reason and reason tells girls that with the aid of a pill, they can go to bed with impunity.

Perhaps this new-found freedom has made them assertive as well as curious about their bodies and their sex organs, and perhaps that accounts for the strange rites which Joannie observed in the darkened room.

Other deans at other colleges have told me that the new morality is giving them fits. I happen to know the dean at Dartmouth, so I called him and asked him how Dartmouth was coping with it. "We no longer try to tell students they can't cohabit," he said. "The embarrassment comes when a roommate makes an official complaint. At that point, you have two bitter enemies, or will have when the other one hears about the complaint. So we split them up and move them as far apart as possible. But for the most part, we hope that roommates can make an accommodation on this problem as they do on others."

I must say I think this is not good enough. Morality is changing before a scientific discovery and I don't know what the new morality will be. Will parents tell children they shouldn't sleep with the opposite sex unless they like them a lot? And in the meantime, there are a lot of still quite young people who came to puberty before science had done its work, or at least before its work was well-known. They must be vast in number. They were taught that they shouldn't sleep with the opposite sex, period. Joannie was one of them. In her eyes, what her roommate was doing was outrageous. Apparently, it is necessary for her to learn tolerance and to be of good will.

But must the colleges come down quite so hard on the side of the new code? If fornication is no longer a bad word, if chastity is a joke, if lewd doesn't mean what it used to mean, what about privacy? Or what about those words of Thomas Jefferson, "a decent respect for the opinion of mankind"? I think the deans of our colleges have yielded too easily. Respect, consideration, thoughtfulness and kindness, privacy and forbearance are still virtues worth inculcating. And when they fall before the strength of the new sexual morality, style loses meaning and, I should think, college dormitories become barns.

I'm sure I sound old-fashioned. My son, David, brought a girl named Alice home one day and Joan and I, having been given suitable warning, took pains to arrange a suitable room for the guest. She stayed a few days, and she was pleasant as well as pretty. When she and David got into her car to drive back to her school, I said politely that I hoped she had been comfortable "up there in that garret room."

"Oh, thank you, Mr. Braden," she replied, with equal politeness. "David and I enjoyed it, but the bed is awfully small for two."

"Never mind," I said to Joan, when the door had been closed and we had exchanged a glance of mutual horror, "the point is there was privacy if she wanted it; style was preserved."

Security Blankets

On the inside back cover of an old scrapbook I kept when I was a boy, there is a rudely drawn map in red ink (a substitute for the blood with which pirates signed their warrants in the books I had been reading).

This map was supposed to reveal the whereabouts of my father's track medals, which I had taken from his bureau drawer, encased in a cigar box, and buried. "Three steps from box elder tree," it says, and then, "six steps towards grocery store."

Steps in what direction, in what size? Alas, the map and the directions were inexact, as my father and I discovered, when, years later, I summoned the courage, or gained the maturity, to tell him what had happened to his track medals.

We dug all around and we failed. The map was useless except as a reminder of what children can do to an adult's security blanket.

"Never mind," my father said. "Don't worry about it," but I remembered his remembering that one of the medals was for a first place in the hundred-yard dash at the Drake relays and I suspect that I deprived him of a security blanket, something he couldn't rationally care about but nevertheless did.

An adult security blanket is important. Suppose that Citizen Kane had kept Rosebud—that sled which turns up in the flames outside the warehouse during the last scene. Suppose he had carted it around with him from one closet to another and one house to another. Wouldn't he have been spared that lifetime of trying to compensate?

That's my theory, and on the basis of the psychology of Citizen Kane, it's a perfectly sound theory. The only thing wrong with it is that in real life, if a man has a desperate need to go to the closet and look at an old sled—or some other symbol of lonely strength and self-sufficiency— he finds, sooner or later, that the children have taken it.

Consider my own symbol. I don't know why I cared so much about that .38 Smith and Wesson revolver. I never used it. I carefully avoided accepting bullets for it. I know that a loaded gun in a house full of children is an invitation to tragedy. And yet, there it was, in my left-hand bureau drawer along with my handkerchiefs, oiled and cleaned, and well, there. And then one day it wasn't there and I cared.

And this despite the fact that none of the memories associated with it were particularly proud. I fired it once at a German officer running down the road, and missed.

And once in Italy's December snows, I used it in a way that is still painful to remember. We had been marching and skirmishing all day and when it got dark we came near a village and the boys in my platoon were elated at the prospect of sleeping indoors.

But somehow the colonel and the majors and the captains all got under roofs ahead of us, and all I could find for my platoon was a tiny white house, occupied by a young Italian family.

I wondered why the young father who stood there barring the door wasn't in the army. Was he a deserter? Or was it that he was home on leave—his wife had a very new baby—when he had been caught by the Allied landing?

He was wearing plain dark trousers and a white shirt and he had a handsome face under his black hair. But there was hatred in the dark eyes and he was adamant in his refusal to let us come in.

So out came the revolver and sometimes at night, still, I have the picture in my head of the man and the woman and the bundled-up baby trudging up the road in the snow while sixteen soldiers move into their house. It is not a pleasing self-portrait for a man to go to bed with. "Don't be silly," I say to myself, "they must have had friends to stay with and we were out of their house the next morning. Other families used to let us move in for a night and they didn't go up the road. So quit thinking of that family disappearing in the snow." But I don't like the picture, and particularly I don't like the one before it—the one of me at the door, pulling the revolver.

Why do I go on about this silly revolver? Obviously, it must have been a security blanket, a symbol of status and also a symbol of a time before I had all this family. It reminds me that I got along, nevertheless, very well.

The loss of most things is merely annoying—combs, socks, money, hairbrushes, ties, razors. Often, to be sure, very annoying, particularly in the morning. You get out of bed, cheerily recounting to yourself that which ought to be done. You make your way to the shower, and then, naked before the mirror, you soap your face with shaving cream, reach out to the right or to the left for the razor on the shelf, and it's not there.

It is the moment when a man feels at his most powerless. He is tricked and defeated and gulled. Right at the beginning of the race saboteurs have caused him to break stride.

So there you are in the bathroom with nothing on and a lot of soap on your face. You can't go out into the hall and shout, "Who took my razor?" because you are naked and if you shout, "Who took my razor?" from behind the closed bathroom door, somebody will say, "Dad's shouting."

On the other hand, there is the soap. If you don't do something soon, the soap will begin to disintegrate. Already it is feeling sticky.

So there is nothing to do but wash it off and dry your face and get dressed and go look for the razor. And when you find it, you have to get partially undressed again, or else shave with your shirt on. There is nothing so disaster prone as shaving with a shirt on.

"Who took my razor?" I cry angrily, as I march from bedroom to bedroom, and girls fly before me through the hall. I buy them razors at Christmas time. I always do. But sooner or later one of them will come, nevertheless, and take mine.

It is, as I say, an annoyance. But the loss of the .38 was something else. One day it was not in its customary place, but for all I know it may on that day have been missing for weeks or even months. A man can raise hell about an annoyance like a missing razor, but a missing security blanket calls for solemnity. Quietly, I asked about the .38. Nobody knew the answer; it was just gone.

In the same mysterious way, I lost my sleeping bag, which was also a link to the past though to a past less long ago. I had lugged that bag over a great many mountain trails in Colorado and California and I treasured it in the true sense of the word, taking pleasure in the fact that it was there.

The sleeping bag disappeared not long after the revolver, and I pined more loudly and openly about it, perhaps because pining for a thing of use seemed more rational and therefore more acceptable than pining for an object of sentimentality.

Though for that matter, the two were really about the same. It had been years since I used that sleeping bag. It was, in fact, in 1966 when the California State Board of Education of which

I was president assaulted Mount Whitney on a dare.

We had been discussing physical education programs, and I had said that I kept in pretty good shape by running a mile every morning. Dr. Maxwell Rafferty, who was the Superintendent of Public Instruction, disagreed with me, as was to be expected from one who presided over a system requiring every schoolchild in the state to participate in physical education for one hour every school day.

I suggested that all nine board members, none of whom exercised one hour per day, were nevertheless in pretty good shape and that to prove it we'd climb the state's highest mountain.

Some of the members were wise enough to have other things to do on the appointed weekend but I was stuck with the challenge because it got into the newspapers and several reporters said they wanted to go along.

I got to the foot of Whitney very late and had to hike at night to catch the party. It was cold and I was exhausted. But my son, David, had been in the advance and when I arrived, there was an air mattress, blown up and out for me, and there was my sleeping bag. The next morning Billy Norris, the Board's vice president and a fellow hiker, had to remind me that lugging an extra sleeping bag to 10,000 feet and then blowing up an air mattress was a thoughtful and loving thing for a fourteen-year-old to do.

So now that sleeping bag was gone, too, and

nothing to do about it. But I mourned, and out loud.

And then one winter evening at dinner, Joannie stood up behind her chair and said she wanted to give a gift to her father on the condition that he would ask no questions about the source of the gift. And I said, "Of course," not knowing what she had in mind. And she produced the sleeping bag from under her chair. At which point David rose, asked for the same condition, and handed me across the table an old beaten-up rusted-out gun. It was recognizable though. It was my .38.

So there they are back in their places, the gun in my drawer, the sleeping bag in my closet, both somewhat the worse for adventures about which I have never inquired, but both effectively fulfilling their purpose as security blankets.

I wonder if on some future winter's eve I'll get back my .22 rifle, my Swiss army knife and—to mention mere nuisances again—the tops to my blue pajamas.

The Love Affair

Sometimes when I see Nancy's love affair, his boots propped on the dining-room table, his motorcycle crash helmet on the floor, his slightly blotched visage confronting me with wary but otherwise expressionless eyes, my mind goes back to that parachute I brought home from Italy.

In Italy, VE Day dawned very hot and the sun beat down mercilessly as we got our gear together and lined up by the trucks which were to carry us on the first stage of the journey home. There was a whole pile of parachutes dumped by the side of the road and there were piles for other kinds of equipment too and the piles grew as more and more soldiers got rid of that which they would no longer need.

But I was in doubt about whether to put my parachute in the pile. A red-faced sergeant, still packing his on his back, made up my mind for me. "Are you going to keep that thing?" I asked.

"Hell, yes," he answered, "I'll give it to my daughter for a wedding dress."

They made parachutes out of real silk in World War II.

So, my parachute has been stored in one basement after another during the years since, a no-doubt moldering symbol of the kind of wedding ceremonies my daughters would choose.

You can visualize the scene. A lovely afternoon in June; gray flannel trousers and white coat; an awning; a glass of champagne. F. Scott Fitzgerald reduced to modest but respectable circumstance.

Alas, it may never be. Nancy is the only one of my daughters who has yet fallen in love and I do not see anywhere in her future the slightest promise for the use of that parachute.

At eighteen, Nancy has without question the classic good looks in the family. Blond, tall, good legs, good figure, large blue eyes, oval face. Add to that a high intelligence—at least she gets the best grades in the family—and a polite but unswerving sureness of purpose. When Nancy was fourteen, my friend Jack Valenti warned me of what was to come, and I have often looked back wistfully upon his advice.

"Tom," he said, in his slight Texas drawl, "I tell you what I'd do if that were my daughter. I'd get myself a damned good shotgun and I'd set out on the front stoop."

I laughed. You can afford to laugh when a girl is fourteen.

Nancy's love affair entered my life about two years ago, having previously entered Nancy's life as a classmate in high school. The first time I saw him he was wearing a dirty red sweater, a pair of pants and boots and had his feet propped up on the table. He did not speak to me then and has seldom spoken to me since, a fact which I have tried, not altogether successfully, to excuse on the grounds that he is embarrassed and shy.

And I know that it is I who make him embarrassed and shy. I cannot help it. I do not like boys who prop their boots on somebody's table; I do not like boys who don't introduce themselves. I know it's old-fashioned; I know that teen-agers are self-conscious and that self-consciousness sometimes reveals itself in seeming rudeness; I know that neither clothes nor manners make a man. But I cannot help it; I do not like boys who seem to have absolutely nothing to do except sit in my dining room or my kitchen and stare at my daughter. In short, and from the start, I did not like Nancy's love affair.

And as I look back on the symbol of the parachute and wonder how I got into the fix I am now in with Nancy, I must say in honesty that the fault is mostly mine. Not liking Nancy's love affair, I made only occasional and not very strenuous efforts to get to know him so that I should like him better. I hoped that even without Valenti's shotgun, he would go away. Any psychiatrist could have told me it was not the thing to do. A father who disapproves of a love affair and who makes his disapproval clear is almost certain to evoke rebellion. In this instance, it went all the way.

Nancy wrote a note of apology and explanation, asserting decision, independence and love.

Joan said, "At least Nancy's note is sweet." I said, " 'Shocking' is a better word; 'maddening,' 'dumfounding,' 'cataclysmic.' "

I disapproved. I strongly disapproved. I think sex assumes responsibility. I recalled Judge Ben B. Lindsay, who shocked the nation during the twenties by proposing what he called companionate marriage. Even Judge Lindsay would have had the couple come to court and obtain sanction for the trial marriage. He knew that sex assumed responsibility.

But as time has passed and temper cooled, I have begun to argue with myself. How long ago did Judge Lindsay propose companionate marriage? Fifty years ago. That was a war ago; a pill ago; a liberation ago. And what, I ask myself, does sex assume responsibility for?

For children, comes the ready answer. But the answer to that is that there won't be any children, or needn't be. Pill.

For physical care, then; for a roof; a bed; board. But Nancy has a roof and a bed and board. She has all that from me, and if I choose not to share them with her any more, she has a job now that she's graduated from high school, and it's a good job and she can pay for all these things on her own. Liberation.

Well, then, I told myself, sex assumes responsibility for marriage. Or so we used to think. But

Nancy does not want to get married. I'm not sure she has even made up her mind to live with her love affair. She is talking about going off to Alaska with him for a month so that she can find out. Marriage, in Nancy's lexicon, is a favor you might be willing to do for your father or mother but only after you have lived with your love affair for quite a long time so as to be sure.

Is there not some reason in her point of view? I ask myself that question. I hate to ask it because my every instinct is to find Nancy's conduct so maddening as to warrant ordering her from the house. But much as I hate to ask the question, I hate the answer more. For the answer—I say to myself, "Be cool now and answer the question"— the answer is "Of course, there is some reason to her point of view."

I saw her point of view most clearly on that Saturday when she lay in bed with a stomach ailment. All day, the love affair, braving me and my unwelcoming air, tiptoed up and down the stairs bringing cups of hot tea from the kitchen. At dusk I went out to get myself some coffee and found him standing over the burner.

"Not hot enough?" I asked, disguising embarrassment with innocuousness.

"She can only take a few sips at a time," he answered. "I have to keep it from getting cold."

"Devotion," I remarked to myself, "is a virtue which does not require the sanction of marriage." Nancy's love affair loved her back.

And yet I must say that if Nancy's point of view prevails, and observation tells me that its adherents are of growing numbers, I fear for the old traditions. I should hate to see them go. Is there any hope for weddings—with or without silk gowns? If a wedding is no longer a necessary or even particularly desirable consequence of a decision by two people to live together, will those who are married be counted as squares? And how shall the census bureau count families? Marriage rates and divorce rates won't mean much any more.

But I think of things I counted as more important. I remember exactly where I was standing and exactly how Joan looked when I persuaded her to set a date for our wedding and I remember exactly where I was standing and exactly how Joan looked when she changed her mind and I had to persuade her again.

And a wedding—isn't it always and no matter of whom a lovely thing? All that hope and kindness and tenderness and coming together? The words of the vow are lovely words as are the friends to look back on, and the official parting from the family. Will girls no longer care to remember that their fathers were nervous and couldn't tie their ties?

I'm less sure about the sex. Two inexperienced people on a wedding night probably do not afford each other a pleasant memory though maybe, in the maturity of later years, it's a funny one. A wedding used to be sanction for maturity suddenly arrived. Nancy's generation may be right in the tacit assumption that it was silly of our generation to assume that maturity came all at once, on the wedding night.

So I don't really know whether to feel sad or angry or just resigned about Nancy. And I am not certain yet whether I am witnessing the coming of a new age or merely a particularly vivid and personal departure from the standards I held dear.

And I'm only kidding about the parachute. I don't care if nobody uses the parachute. Let it rot in the basement. Except, I was thinking just the other evening about how Susan happened to go to Dartmouth. I went to Dartmouth. I'm on the board of trustees there. One night after I got home from a trustee meeting, I was standing in Susan and Joannie's room telling them about how the trustees had voted to admit girls. There had been a long argument with many of the trustees vigorously opposed, and I said I had fought hard for the girls.

And then I went down the hall to go to bed and the next morning Joannie told me that after I left, Susan said, "Well, that settles it. I'll have to go to Dartmouth." And Joannie said, "Why?" And Susan answered, "Poor Dad. Somebody has to."

Say, you don't suppose that when Susan has her love affair, she might want to use that old parachute down in the basement?

The Anti-Saloon League and Me

When I was a small boy in Dubuque, Iowa, I accompanied my mother and my grandmother one evening to hear a lecture by the Reverend Wayne B. Wheeler of the Anti-Saloon League.

Mr. Wheeler was a large, florid man with white hair and an old-fashioned style of oratory. He boomed at the respectable citizens gathered in the basement of the First Congregational Church, and after he boomed, he pled: "For the sake of the soldiers, dead on the field of battle; for the sake of the unborn babies stretching out their heavenly arms, woncha, woncha give up rum?"

Mother wrote a description of the meeting for H. L. Mencken's *American Mercury* and reported that the Reverend Wheeler pled first with the organist of the Second Baptist Church, then with the rector of St. John's.

"He induces," she wrote, "the whole company to stand in groups and for an assortment of rea-

121

sons: 'the WCTU ladies because they are the mothers of the Anti-Saloon League. Oh, what a story could be told about them.'"

Mother thought the Reverend Wheeler was funny, but she wrote her article under a pseudonym. It would have been almost as cruel to let Grandmother know that any child of hers would make fun of the Anti-Saloon League as it would have been to let her know that any child of hers would take a drink, which, of course, Mother did.

I think of the relationship between my mother and my grandmother on the subject of the taboo because it seems to me a nearly perfect mirror of the relationship between my children and me. My grandmother thought alcohol an abomination. My mother disagreed. I think drugs an abomination. My children disagree. "One generation passeth away and another generation cometh" did not adequately warn us that the roof was about to fall in.

It began with innocence. I went upstairs one evening in the fall of 1967, and passing my son's room, I heard low voices. Thinking to exchange a pleasantry or two, I knocked twice and entered. A remarkable scene confronted me. In a circle on the floor, their legs folded beneath them, their eyes, I later reflected, looking up at me with startled awareness of intrusion, was a group of boys, my son among them, engaged in what appeared to be some form of worship.

On the floor in the center of the circle was a tall candle. In the center of the circle also was a candlestick containing incense, and on two side tables outside the circle, incense also burned.

"What in the world," I asked, "are you doing?" Ah, the age of innocence. To think that only a few years ago, I could, upon witnessing such a scene, ask such a question.

"Just burning a little incense, Dad," David answered, and I find it almost unbelievable now to think that, while I wasn't quite satisfied with the answer, I did not thunder nor accuse.

Nor know. A group of fifteen-year-old boys engaged in some strange rite—was it an initiation ceremony for some neighborhood or high-school secret society? I remembered that at about the same age, my friends and I were signing secret pacts of alliance with blood drawn from each other's arms.

I mentioned the ceremony to Joan that evening. "What do you suppose was going on?" She was as innocent as I.

Our awakening did not come for several years, and when it came, it was rude. I try to take telephone calls in the middle of the night because they are never pleasant calls and taking them seems a father's rather than a mother's role. But this call was more than unpleasant.

"Dad," David said, "I'm in jail."

I tried to be calm and to get all the details and at the end of the conversation, I recovered sufficiently to say something cheerful. "Well, other people have spent a night in jail and recovered and you can recover too. So buck up, and I'll get right on this in the morning." Something like that.

But it was a shock, a serious physical shock.

Anybody who tells you that you can take a call from a son who is in jail and not hurt for weeks afterward is a person who doesn't care about his children.

Also, it posed a moral issue. A father likes to thinks of himself as both the protector of his children and defender of the upright. A son who is in jail for violating the law is a problem in allegiance.

Allegiance once determined, the cost of it must be borne. David had been driving down Highway 101 in Orange County, California, in an old Volkswagen, accompanied by a friend. The Volkswagen had a defective taillight, and the California Highway Patrol had stopped the boys, searched their pockets and the car's floor, and finally found a few grains of marijuana in the car's ashtray. The problem, a lawyer friend in Los Angeles explained, was to convince the prosecuting attorney that his duty might be fulfilled by permitting David to plead guilty to the crime for which he had been stopped, i.e., the defective taillight. My friend knew a good man, but the fee would be high: about fifteen hundred dollars.

Looking back, I'm not absolutely sure that what I did was the right thing to do. As I did it, I felt sad. All that money David had saved since he was a little boy: allowance money, Christmas gift money, jackpot money for catching the biggest fish on the Oceanside fishing boat—it came altogether to about fifteen hundred dollars. I drew it out of David's savings account and sent it off to the lawyer.

Was I wrong? I said to myself at the time, "He'll have to grow up someday, and the quickest way to help him grow up is to make him understand that he is responsible for his own errors." But three months in jail? I couldn't stand it, even if he could. If I ever have a spare fifteen hundred dollars, I shall give it to David.

The lawyer earned his fee. David was sentenced to serve three successive weekends in the Orange County jail. His friend, who didn't have fifteen hundred dollars, served the mandatory term. David was embarrassed and angry, partly at the loss of his fifteen hundred dollars, but mostly because I had arranged for him to be treated differently.

So that was my awakening. What did it teach me? I am sorry to say that I was left with ambivalence. In the first place, I think the experience probably persuaded the two boys that they ought to take a whisk broom to the car before they set out on a highway. But will it teach them not to smoke marijuana? No more than the Reverend Wayne B. Wheeler or the eighteenth amendment to the Constitution persuaded my mother to "give up rum."

And in the second place, the more I looked into the mores of marijuana and the laws against it, the more I became convinced that the legal penalty for breaking the law is far worse than the crime. Not only that, but it seems to me that there is justice in the prevalent view of the young that they are the victims of bad law and of policemen who enforce bad law selectively.

Marijuana has become a generational symbol. In 1973, more than three hundred thousand Americans were arrested for possessing it and eighty-six percent of them, according to the FBI, were under the age of twenty-six.

"The only way we can get rid of longhaired kids on the upper peninsula," a police chief in Michigan told me, "is to let the word get around that we'll follow them until we spot a traffic violation and throw them into jail after we find the stuff." This is not a drug abatement program; it is a youth abatement program and I am against it.

What we have done is to create a scapegoat minority, consisting of young people with long hair and old cars. Few experts hold that moderate use of marijuana is any more dangerous to the human body than moderate use of alcohol or tobacco. Yet the sixty million Americans who smoke cigarettes and the one hundred million who use alcohol can do so with impunity. In every state in the union except Oregon, those who are caught with marijuana risk a jail sentence.

Thus my ambivalence. I felt it most strongly on the day in 1969 when some of my children marched in the Great Moratorium. It was said to be the largest crowd in American history, though the television cameras, awed, it is hard to believe now, by Spiro Agnew, ignored it. The marchers were mostly young, assembled in generational protest and many of those who witnessed it will bear testimony that the symbol of protest was marijuana. The air reeked of the stuff. A great sickly sweet cloud hung over the Washington Mall.

"The march itself was like a river," Joannie told me, "and we were all just drops in the river. All those people caring; we will have an effect." Joannie had carried a flower for a dead soldier and marched all day to toss it against a wall. She was wearing blue jeans with red hearts sewn around the ankles and a blue workshirt and boots, and her curly hair was too long and she seemed to me infinitely good and trusting and believing, like most of the people in her river.

I had gone down to watch her river run and spread itself out around the Washington Monument when it had finished running. The drops in Joannie's river were lying on blankets, smoking marijuana.

And then I had walked over to the Justice Department building where a small band of the unruly were trying to plant a Viet Cong flag on Mr. Mitchell's building, and I had seen another river, this one of Washington police, wearing gas masks and advancing, rubber truncheoned in solid phalanx.

It seemed to me there was not much doubt about which was the more powerful group. Ambivalence bothered me again. On the one side were my children, wearing blue jeans and boots and workshirts and long hair, protesting the laws and breaking them by smoking marijuana.

On the other side were those policemen in gas masks and behind them, the authority of Mr. Nixon's White House.

They were good-looking, short-haired, blue-suited, striped-tied, flag-lapeled, those people in the White House, and they weren't wasting their time reading Herman Hesse's novels, or smoking pot or marching in a parade. Jeb Stuart Magruder, Dwight Chapin, Bob Haldeman. When were my children going to start looking and behaving like them?

And if they didn't start pretty soon to look and behave like them, would they ever grow up to be really succesful and respected and substantial—like John Mitchell or Maurice Stans?

The two rivers couldn't meet. Joannie learned some months later, at the time of the Cambodian invasion, that Mr. Nixon had himself gone to talk to students at the Lincoln Memorial—had slipped out in the middle of the night to do so—had run across a boy from Syracuse University, and had asked about the football team, in sports-page language: "How are the Orangemen?" She reacted in disbelief. "Was he spaced out?" she wanted to know.

Later, of course, I realized my mistake. I had mistaken the style of the White House—the business suits, the haircuts, the abstention from drugs, the earnest straight looks—for virtue.

My children smoked dope and dressed badly by White House standards. But they believed in their country just as much as the men in the White House, and I think it's fair to say they were more honest.

I say to my children, "You may not smoke marijuana in this house because it is against the law."

But I am not a true believer. I cannot bring myself to plead with them as the Reverend Wheeler
pled with me. And though they have respected
my wishes and commands and do not smoke
marijuana in the house, I would not be surprised
to learn that from time to time they smoke it elsewhere. The whole thing is unsatisfactory. I don't
like not knowing where I stand.

And I blame my ambivalence on marijuana for
the fact that I did not go on full alert against
other and more dangerous experiments. After
David's arrest, I should have become a narrow-
eyed, suspicious, case-hardened parent. But I
didn't. Not until Elizabeth's birthday party.

I remember Elizabeth's birthday party very
well because it caught me by such surprise. Suddenly the house was filled with people, people
upstairs and downstairs and in the kitchen and
the basement, people of fourteen, fifteen, sixteen,
of both sexes, consuming quantities of Coke, behaving, as far as I could see, perfectly well. It
was just that there were so many of them. And
every time the door opened, more of them poured
in.

I spoke sharply to Joan, who spoke sharply in
return. "I didn't know you were going to have
the whole school here," I said.

"You knew perfectly well," she answered, "because I told you that Elizabeth wanted to invite
her class, and you agreed."

I made a mental note never again to permit a
child to invite a "class." The child may think it
democratic but a child doesn't know the difference

between democracy and mob rule. And just as I was reflecting on this minor lesson, I noticed that some members of the "class" were behaving oddly.

I looked again. They *were* behaving oddly. They were drunk, or they seemed to be drunk. That boy over there by the fireplace, for example, talking very slowly, lurching a little; he was sleepy drunk; the kind of drunk one remembers from all-night parties at college fraternity houses.

There was no liquor. I had taken that precaution. All securely locked in the basement. Then what hadn't I done? Suddenly the truth dawned. Sleepy drunk. I bolted up the stairs to the bathroom and went straight to the medicine chest. The sleeping pills were gone.

I went through everything—bottles of tetra-this and chlory-that, anti-bug bite pills, pills to dry up colds. "Joan," I said, returning to the foot of the stairs, "weren't there some sleeping pills in the medicine cabinet? Because if there were, there aren't now."

Joan was not absolutely sure. But she was pretty sure. So was I. Questioned, the "drunken" members of the class denied knowledge. I called parents, rounded up cars and drivers and got them home. The experience frightened me more than I have ever been frightened before or since and humbled me and made me resolve.

There are not, in our medicine chest now, any pills at all. No penicillin; nothing left over from the last prescription for the last complaint. I threw them all away that evening and as fast as any member of the family recovers from whatever illness has caused us to purchase pills, I throw out what's left in the bottle.

Why, after LSD and after speed and after all those other abominations which David's age group tried and eventually rejected, why should Elizabeth's age group try sleeping pills? There was that brief respite in-between, that time when drugs were out, and only marijuana was in, and then just as we began to let our guard down, we have fifteen-year-old children going around talking about "reds."

I have no ambivalence whatever about where I stand. I have gone the whole way. I will thunder more loudly than the Reverend Wheeler thundered at me and I have become not only narrow-eyed but hard-nosed. "Let me see what's in your pockets" is a legitimate demand at our house, and must be honored by anyone below the age of eighteen.

In fact, I have become so suspicious of the possibility that one of my children might sneak pills into the house, or that the latest fad at the school will turn up some other killer I haven't yet learned about that I tend, on the subject of more common evils, to be rather tolerant.

Alcohol, for example. We all know the Reverend Wheeler was partly right. We know it can be an abomination. But we also know that some of us at least have learned to handle it so that it is a pleasure and we live in hope that our children will learn too. "Nancy," Joan remarked on a recent evening, "came home from work this afternoon, went straight to the liquor closet and poured herself a huge glass of wine. I think you should speak to her."

A banality began to form itself upon my lips and then I suddenly realized that I enjoyed giving voice to it. "A glass of wine," I said, "won't kill her." I said it with feeling.

Unpoor and Unrich

On the desk in front of me as I write these lines is a long thin slip of paper marked at the top in attention-contriving open-spaced lettering, "Notice of Insufficient Funds." Down below are printed demarcations with computer-typed details: "Number of Checks Presented, (1); Amount of Checks presented (2.50); Amount of Insufficient Balance (98.27).

The slip of paper was not on my desk when I left this morning. Moreover, it is not my slip of paper. It must have been neatly propped against the little oriental box on my desk by the addressee. The addressee is Mary Braden, my oldest daughter. She has performed what I am certain she regards as her exact duty.

There is no accompanying note, no instruction, no apology. The piece of paper speaks for itself. It says, first of all, "Dad, please pay up." But it says a lot of other things too, and as I look at it, my mind goes back to a lifetime of overdrafts and worry and borrowing and having eight children. It's not the ninety-eight twenty-seven I mind so much. Ninety-eight twenty-seven is a possible sum, and doubtless some oversight on my part has given Mary the right to remind her father, in the famous words of Daniel Webster, "to replenish my account." Mary is an honest girl and also a thrifty one. Nevertheless, something about this reminder tells me what my children think of me, and perhaps, of what all children think of all fathers.

A checkwriter, that's what I have become; a tall figure, aging slightly, sometimes ill-tempered; no longer fast at touch football; somewhat of an embarrassment at singles tennis and now, at long last, easy to pass and defeat in the mile run. But despite these deficiencies, possessed of money. "Dad, I need five dollars." "Dad, there's a note from my college; I put it on your desk." "Dad, can I have my allowance?" "Dad, Joannie and I want to go to the movies." "Dad . . ." Sometimes I could shout and sometimes I do. Sometimes I could cry though I have not done that, but all the time, I worry. Joan says, "Don't worry," and I do.

I have a cataract on my right eye. It must be removed and when the doctor tells me about it, I am dumfounded. I thought cataracts in eyes were for people who are eighty. "Why?" I demand. "What causes this?" He explains that even children can have cataracts and that anyone who lives long enough will eventually have one. But he admits that most people who have cataracts are considerably older than I.

Diabetes, he tells me, or a tendency thereto, is one possible cause. I tell him I have never had a trace of it. "Another," he says, "and quite apart from natural aging, is stress. Do you feel any stress?" "Yes," I said. "I need money."

And why not? The one thing that a father of eight children must somehow manage to find; the one thing he cannot possibly do without, and which love and affection, care and patience, attention, kindness, interest and ability to help with arithmetic cannot possibly replace is money. "Put money in thy purse," said Iago in his famous speech to Roderigo. I first read that line when I was fifteen. But I must have supposed that what it meant was "Get some money from Dad." My children suppose the same.

On a rough calculation, I have taken in during a working life which began the moment the war ended in 1945, about a million, five hundred and fifty thousand dollars. It comes out to an average of about fifty thousand dollars per year, and I ought to feel proud of myself that it's far more than the average of lifetime earnings. According to the Census Bureau, the average income for all persons in the United States from the age of twenty-five until death is $347,859. Those who have had four years of college, as I did, average $580,000. So, I've done well, even perhaps very well.

But I don't tell myself that. I am broke, and I am nearly always broke. Moreover, I have absolutely nothing to show for that million and a half dollars, except the partly paid for house I live in, a car, and such items as books, clothes, furniture—things which even the poor can boast of. Except for one thing—I have eight children. And that, of course, is where the money went.

It went first of all on food. I can remember when the grocery bill was $100 a month, and then $200, and now I try to think we manage on $600, but we really don't because I have ceased to include the milk bill, which is separate and comes to about $100 per month. "Drink water," I keep saying to Tommy and Nicky and their friends who come home with them after school. "Water is very good for you." And Tommy looks up from the sideboard where he is spreading something very thick and gooey, and says, "Dad, have you ever tried a peanut butter and jelly sandwich with a glass of nice thick water?"

And I say to myself, "Well, I do save money on Coca-Cola, which I long ago barred from the house along with ginger ale, root beer, Fresca and all the other money-eaters which children love. I barred them, not so much because I object to them per se, but because it was impossible to keep them. A case of Coca-Cola on a Saturday was gone on the same Saturday. There would be a faintly surprised glance at me: "Where'd you get the Coke, Dad?" And the next time I looked, the case was gone.

So, I try to ignore the milk bill. I mean, I try to forget that it's bigger than it ought to be and I concentrate instead on the food bill, which is more susceptible to change. Mostly upward, I agree. But there is one thing which can be done about it. It came to me the summer of 1973, when lamb chops were selling at eighty cents each. I remember the price of lamb chops because I was standing in front of the meat counter at an A&P market when suddenly an old man standing next to me turned and fixed me with a glittering eye that would have done credit to the Ancient Mariner. "Sixty-eight years," he said in a kind of wail, "man and boy I've lived in this town and in all that time I never seen anything like this."

He continued berating the Nixon administration, the grain deal with Russia, the middlemen and the food markets, addressing himself exclusively to me, and his voice rose, so that it was embarrassing and I turned aside somewhere between soap and kitchen utensils. There, lying neatly stacked on a bottom shelf, I saw something I had not thought about for many years—package upon package of dried white beans.

A long-forgotten image came to mind—Grandmother's kitchen on a Thursday afternoon when I came to mow her lawn. Those white beans soaking in a huge pot to be ready for Saturday night supper. If Grandmother could do it, why not I?

It was thus I learned about a minor weapon against inflation and also about the approbation of daughters which every father seeks. As a group, if fathers can be so called, two goals are paramount. First, to provide: fathers actually enjoy seeing their children eat. Second, the admiration of daughters. Sons are not admirers. After the age of puberty, if a son has not rebelled, a father begins to wonder why. But to call a daughter on the long distance telephone, and to hear her say, "Is this my father?" in a joyous and excited surprise—this is what fathers live for.

To bring home a sack of dried beans fulfills the need to provide, but, of course, it will get you no cheers. If you follow my recommendation, you will go further.

There was a recipe for Boston baked beans in the kitchen cookbook and another on the back of the cellophane wrapper. One called for dark beer, the other for tomato juice. One called for molasses, the other for maple syrup. One recommended boiling the beans, the other warned against it. But both were in agreement on soaking the beans overnight, cooking them in hot water until soft, adding the tomato juice-beer, the molasses-maple syrup, mustard and salt before baking six to eight hours at 250 degrees.

It made a marvelous meal for a family of ten, at a cost of less than the price of two lamb chops. I have repeated the experiment once a week ever since and always with success. The fact that the meal has historical interest (Great-grandmother is a good topic of conversation in any family), that the process takes a couple of days, thus permitting trepidation and suspense (before baking, the beans always look as though something had gone wrong), that the consumption can be viewed as a thrust at inflation and vengeance against those responsible—all this helps to make a father feel worthy and actually does cut down a little bit on the grocery bill.

I wish I knew equally good ways to cut the expense of equally important things. Clothes, for example. But we have been very lucky about clothes. The only one in the family who spends too much on clothes is Joan, and she pays for them out of her own salary.

The children, growing up on a beach, didn't care very much what they put on their backs and what they put on their backs didn't cost much. Not until we moved from California back to Maryland did any of them wear shoes except under protest, and I saved a lot of money by not protesting very much. The change was more expensive than it should have been because the smaller children, having formed the habit of going barefoot, tended to lose their shoes in Maryland. But, after the first winter, they grew accustomed to the new climate and the bills went down.

And then about the time they got to be teenagers, they adopted the uniform of their generation. Blue jeans and nothing but blue jeans. I made some mild protests, particularly to the girls. "Blue jeans," I said, "are boring. Why don't you put on a dress?" But secretly, I told myself I was saving money. What if the styles of the late sixties and early seventies had been different? What if five girls wanted to wear five dresses? What if they wanted to wear different dresses each day? Thank God for blue jeans.

I think of other occasions and items on which, over the year, great outlays have been made. It seems to me that I have bought enough bicycles to equip an army and enough Christmas presents to make a mockery of religion. I can remember one Christmas in California when there were so many presents under the tree and around the tree and sprawled out into the far corners of a room that even the children were sickened by it, and halfway through the ceremony of opening them, the younger ones began to cry out of sheer fatigue. I remember Tommy saying, "I don't want to open any more presents." That was the last Christmas that was anything like that. Joan and I had made a mistake, and we knew it and the children knew it, and we never made the mistake again. I think of the mistake, even now, with revulsion.

A man can do something—however slight—about the food bill; he can be lucky about the clothing bill; he can shake himself about ways his family is spending money unnecessarily. But there is one expense about which, as far as I know, he can do nothing at all. It is the biggest expense; the one for which he vainly saves and for which he might even consider stealing. There is no way of avoiding this expense. He can say to his children, "I can't do it," but there is no way he can say that without suffering the knowledge that whatever he has done for his children, it was not enough to do. I refer, of course, to college, without which no child can ever expect to earn very much money. College is not essential to success. Success is doing well at something and knowing in your own heart that you did well. College is a help to success but it is essential only to earning money.

I wish the figures did not prove that statement

to be so true. In 1973, the mean income of all men in the United States twenty-five years or over was $10,943. For those who had been to college one to three years, it was $12,515; for those who had graduated from college, $15,974; for those who had five or more years of college and graduate school, it was $18,555.

Is it crass of me to want to give my children the opportunity to earn more than the mean? Then so be it. I should feel guilty unless I tried. And so they are going to college, or at least all but one of those who are of college age are going, along with twenty-five percent of their peers. The drain on their father is great, so great as to be almost indescribable. And as each child comes of college age, it grows harder and harder to share with them the boundless joy which comes from the notices of admissions officers.

"Dad, I've been admitted." The voice is a pealing bell. But for me, the words are laden with foreboding. They translate as follows: "Dad, next year you will have to find five thousand more." Or make it four, or three. College charges are almost nowhere less than that and they are going up, like everything else, only faster.

I don't think private colleges are giving sufficient thought to the fact that they are rapidly becoming institutions for the very rich and the very poor. Many of them won't even admit it. And state institutions are on the same path. Their tuitions are going up too, although from a lower base. If they follow the lead of the private colleges and the wisdom of the educational establishment, they will shortly be beyond the means of their principal constituency, that is, the great American middle class.

College officials answer the charge that they are turning aside the middle class by pointing to government insured loans. I can't believe any college official ever tried to get one. What they will discover, if they do, is that the child of anyone who earns more than $15,000 per year is extremely unlikely to be eligible for such a loan. Anyone who earns more than $20,000 can forget about applying. Oh, I know that if you have more than one child to put through college, adjustments are in order. College officials are supposed to add up your gross income, make deductions according to the number of children in the family, and then determine whether your child is eligible for scholarship aid.

Put yourself in the position of one of those college officials. Here is an applicant from a family which earns less than $10,000 annually. Here is another applicant from a family which earns $30,000 annually. Which family would you want to help?

My own way out has been to borrow from life insurance, from banks, from friends—anybody I can borrow from.

The children work—as I worked when I went to college. But when I went to college, tuition was four hundred dollars per year. Today it's four thousand. Working your way through college is no longer possible.

I wish tuition and board and room were the

total bill. My daughter Joannie says her class-mates constantly ask her, "Why don't you have any money?"

Their attitude is realistic. "You're here," they seem to be saying, "If you're here, you must have money. So why can't you afford to go to the movies?"

I went up to Dartmouth recently to a trustees' meeting. Susan was at Dartmouth, and Joannie came over from Bennington, to which she had transferred when she couldn't stand sex education at Antioch. We had breakfast together for two days running, and in between meetings, we took long walks and had fun. We were all leaving—Susan for classes, Joannie to catch the bus for Bennington and I to catch the airplane home—when the girls mentioned money. I opened my wallet and I found a five-dollar bill and four ones. So I took out the four ones and I handed them each two.

There were reverberations. My friend Charles McLane who teaches government at Dartmouth had talked to my daughters, and when I appeared for the next meeting of the trustees, he talked to me.

"Braden," he said, "I think you're being a little old-fashioned. You exalt the value of self-dependence, but forget about inflation. A couple of dollars when you and I were at Dartmouth was spending money. Three dollars bought a whole case of beer. Today it hardly pays the price of a movie."

Charley explained the facts of life. "I should

think thirty-five dollars a week would be about right," he advised, "for spending money."

I did not quarrel with my old friend, whom I greatly admire. He wouldn't believe the truth. The truth is that after tuition and board and room and books and travel, I don't have thirty-five dollars for any child. They're lucky when I have two.

The Good Life

You have this idea in your head all your life that you will have a house which will be pleasant and serene and roomy enough to accommodate friends, and with a place outside large enough for the children to play.

And you hope the children will bring other children. It is satisfying to think that they have friends; they're out there playing baseball or they're in the living room, squatting on the floor, playing that game you bought one of them last Christmas.

Can Tommy's friend stay all night? Of course he can stay all night, his mother willing. A certain pleasure swells the chest. Being host, or watching your children be host is a substantial, solid pleasure. It's the good life.

And then somewhere along the line—is it the age of fifteen? Sixteen? Seventeen?—it is no good any more. The pride is gone; the hospitality is gone; you are no longer a host; you are being used and so is your hospitality and your liquor and your furniture and your reputation.

It has all been seized by a gang, consisting of your own child or children plus boys or girls whose parents you know, whom you knew as younger girls and boys, and knew as nice girls and boys.

And what are they doing now? They are sitting in your living room, staring at one another, and once in a while chortling to each other, and they are waiting for you to go.

And when you have gone, they intend to drink your liquor; they intend to investigate your bathroom to see whether you have left a pill or two they can swallow; they intend, at the very least, to raid the icebox, and they will leave the kitchen a mess, put their muddy feet up on the newly upholstered chairs, light a fire in the fireplace and spray sparks on the rug, insert a knife blade into a locked door, and open it, just to see what you have locked up; they intend to take a book from your shelf if it happens to interest them and they are making no mental notes to bring it back; they intend to take your car and go for a ride, and if they dent a fender they will lie about it; they will leave your house a mess; and they will do all this because they resent your house and your hospitality and, most of all, they resent you.

It took me a long time to know that this was true. I couldn't believe it. I kept thinking each time it happened, that each time it happened was an aberration; that some unwanted and intruding stranger had disrupted a gathering of good and upright friends, or that it was an accident; somebody who is normally gentle had been seized by too much alcohol and had behaved in a fashion so shameful that I could count on its never happening again.

But it isn't so. There is a time in the life of a man and a woman, between childhood and adulthood, between dependence and responsibility, between desire and the ability to cope with it, between wanting something and deciding to earn it, when the human being, physically grown and emotionally childish, is a very dangerous animal.

Naturally, the animal snarls at larger, more secure and more peaceful animals. It resents them. "Unconsciously" is perhaps a little strong. I like to think it's unconscious because experience proves that a few years bring a change, and that the change is complete. But I'm not so sure that it's truly unconscious. That stare which greets you when you enter a room of seventeen-year-olds is truly hostile, out of a sense of danger perhaps, for the discovery of some secret or the jeopardy of some plan, out of jealousy perhaps, at the possible departure of the car; but nonetheless, and quite clearly, hostile.

When I discovered that it was true, I tried camaraderie; I tried offering a drink; I tried discussion—topics of the day, sports, politics, style. It helps a little but is by no means an insurance policy. When I can't sleep at three in the morning, and walk down to the kitchen to get a glass of milk, I face, despite the camaraderie, a distinct possibility of witnessing chaos. It is also possible—why didn't I put the key in my pocket?—that the car is gone.

For the last couple of years I have been examining those who belong to Nancy's gang. I have learned the following: First, their hostility is both tribal and generational. It is not individual. In the army we used to say of a certain type of man, "He is a shirt-giver." It was the highest praise one could bestow, and it meant just what it said—that in a pinch, such a man would give you his shirt.

The members of Nancy's gang, I have learned, are often shirt-givers to each other, protecting each other, doing each other kindnesses, walking the last mile for each other.

Nor, I think, does each invididual member of Nancy's gang feel individual hostility toward me. It is only as a group that the hostility asserts itself. For example, Nancy's friend, Phillip, is, as a member of the gang, a menace to both peace and property. One day last summer, having learned from Nancy that Phillip was interested in movies, I mentioned a recent film I had enjoyed and tried to talk to him about a review which I had read and with which I disagreed.

It was a mistake, or so I thought at the time. For I had approached Phillip as he was sitting among the gang in the living room, silent and waiting for me to leave. In response to my overture, he murmured something or other, both unintelligible and final. I walked away, rebuffed.

But last Christmas vacation when the gang were

again reoccupying their summer's lair, Phillip came over one evening quite alone. Seeking me out, he produced, embarrassedly, and looking off to the side as he spoke, "a book on the film which I thought might interest you." He disappeared, almost before I could recover sufficiently to express my thanks, and the next time I saw him, there he was again in the living room, surrounded by his fellows, glaring at me with suspicion.

It is not I, then; not I, as a person, whom Phillip resents but I as a member of a generation, a member of an older, bigger, more prosperous and powerful gang.

Phillip's behavior points toward a truth which mitigates the harsh truth about the mysteriously allotted time span during which children are animals. This truth is that the animals will change into human beings again. It is beginning to happen to Nancy's friend Phillip. I have watched it happen to David and Mary and Susan and Joannie. It happens almost literally overnight. One day they make me grind my teeth at night. (The dentist says teeth grinding at night is quite common among parents of teen-age children.) The next day they are suddenly neat, clean, responsible, and with their hair combed.

I have thought long and hard about what causes a child to change from an animal into a human being, and what causes him to change so rapidly. I have discussed the problem with those who have had animals in their care—with college presidents, for example, and with Ethel Kennedy, who must run a kind of animal farm.

They have recognized the phenomenon too but they have given me advice and explanation either incapable of proof or too general to be worthwhile. Ethel says you have to talk constantly with the animals, develop understanding and mutual trust. That's kind—as Ethel is. But I know it doesn't always work for her or for me.

I have a different theory. I think it's the money supply. I mean just that. What changes or at least helps to change an animal into a human being is the money supply. If I had it to do all over again, I would not have permitted the following:

I would not have given David the money to take a trip around the world, even though it was very little money for a trip around the world.

I would not have given Joannie an allowance that summer when she looked as though she hadn't bathed and was running around with that boy whose hair was so long that everybody wondered if he had a face.

I would not have put money in Mary's bank account the year she was at the University of California, rioting against the Bank of America.

It has taken me four children out of eight to learn the secret: which is, the moment they become animals, cut off the money supply.

Cut it off totally. Don't have any money when asked. Don't send money to the college, or to the college bank. Demand the exact change for sudden departures from the norm, like "Dad, I need money for a haircut," or even, "Mother wants me to go to the grocery store. Do you have some money?" Get the grocery store receipt and measure it against the change you receive. Every dollar you can possibly withhold will make the change from animal to human being more rapid and certain.

But the advice must be taken absolutely literally. You must not deceive yourself into thinking that by the proper expenditure you can bring about the change, as I deceived myself, for example, with David.

Sometime during the summer after he graduated from high school, David decided that he did not want to go to college. I was disappointed and expressed my disagreement from time to time, listing the reasons why I thought college essential and asking for reasons why he had decided against it. "College," David replied, "is your bag, Dad."

But he never told me what his bag was, and it is only now, in retrospect, that I realize that what David really wanted to be was a hippie. I do not use the word in a wholly derogatory sense. I understand the political implication of refusal to join a society mobilized at the time to beat up a lot of poor farmers in Vietnam. I understand the social implications of choosing passive observation of that society rather than participating in it. I am even prepared to imagine that there may be something quite beautiful about being freaked out on dope, not bothering to wear shoes, letting one's hair grow, and simply not caring at all.

But I do not understand the economics of it. After David decided to be a hippie, he came home from school, put on a pair of blue jeans, took his shoes off, and sat around the house. He didn't need much money; in fact, he needed so little that I didn't notice that he needed some.

I worried more about his doing nothing, and that was how I fell into the trap of permitting him to be a real, organized hippie, banded together with other hippies. He said he'd like to go around the world, and I, thinking that to do something was better than nothing, reflecting that he knew two languages and might put them to account, reflecting also that seeing the ancient monuments, or the art museums or the terrains of foreign lands might stir curiosity to learn, decided to come up with the money.

So David departed on a trip around the world, by which I mean that with unerring instinct he headed straight for those parts of the world where other teen-age boys and girls with long hair and no shoes sit and smoke dope and stare, and feel the proper vibes with each other. I don't think he ever saw an art museum or looked at an ancient monument. That would have been "my bag."

Nor did he ever really get all the way around the world. He ran out of money and worked for a while in a vineyard in France. He "had it made" for another while with a matron twice his age who picked him up on the road. He contracted pneumonia and spent some time in a hospital in Iran. He learned the names and ways of the streets of Kabul. He bought and sold rugs with marginal success.

I envied his experience. I reflected that I had never had a similar one and that now it was too late—I had missed the action. I wondered, when David came home, what would he do?

And I was not long in learning. He came home wearing a pair of French work pants, heavy work shoes and a silk turban which he wound around his enormous growth of bushy red hair. He made himself comfortable in one of the bedrooms. And he sat.

After a while, I said, "I thought you would mature." He said, "You want me to mature in the way you think is mature. I've matured in the way I think is mature."

It was then that I hit upon the only weapon left in my arsenal. It was then that I cut off the money supply.

Oh, I suppose there is a stronger weapon. David was twenty-one. I could have kicked him out of the house, forbade him a meal. And I suppose that in the short history of the war between hippie children and straight parents, it has somewhere been done. But it must be a terrible experience, casting a pall upon the years to come, destroying family and affection and shared pride.

My way was less dramatic and there was no confrontation. I simply didn't have any money when asked—no money for cigarettes, no money for gasoline, no money for beer, no money for a movie, no money to go to the places where a silk turban is much admired.

And so, David has a job now. He gets up at six, works hard, and earns substantial pay. He looks better. I think he feels better. He has abandoned the silk turban and he ties his hair in a tight knot behind the neck, as in portraits of the young Thomas Jefferson.

I enjoyed having him around the last summer he was with us. And his friends too who worked with him on his construction job. Sometimes they would come over to our house on Saturday nights and sit in the living room and play records and talk.

It gave me a pleasant feeling. It's the good life. I would walk into the living room and say, "Hi, everybody, would you like some beer?"

The Garden of Eden

Like a lot of my contemporaries, I grew up thinking that the sex role of a man was to chase a woman, and I am jealous of my children, who know better.

A girl, in the lexicon of my generation, was to be protected. So a girl had a room of her own; a girl didn't call a boy on the telephone; a girl's dormitory was carefully guarded by large-bosomed, old ladies in large hats, and there were strict rules about visitors and about signing in and signing out.

But, of course, sex implied that the defenses were overrun, that the protection failed. Therefore, sex was a chase and an assault. "Dartmouth's in town again; run girls run," I learned as a freshman and in a society of men which—except for unfulfilled desire—was self-sufficient and quite happily so, the word "girl" was made subconsciously synonymous with the word "victim."

It was the same in the army. One heard the lectures about the dangers of gonorrhea and syphilis and accepted the issue of protective equipment. For the attack, of course.

I was in my mid-twenties before I learned that chase and attack was not the sole prerogative of the male, and I remember where I learned it. It was at the Cavendish Hotel on Jermyn Street in London. The Cavendish was a pretty rundown place during World War II, barren and dusty, staffed by surly pensioners, containing in some of the rooms occasional mementos of a bright and glittering past. The famous Rosa Lewis, mistress to Edward VII, proprietress to rich British and American escapists between the wars, sat in the front parlor, her feet upon a cushion, her dog, Kippy, at her side. Rosa dressed in the 1910 style, ankle-length skirts of good cloth and much lace at the throat. Often she slept, and often when she awoke to greet some son of a World War I guest, she would awaken and her ashen and ancient cheeks would suddenly glow with the excitement of a memory imparted by her dream. The blue eyes would flash: "We took off all her clothes," Rosa would chant, "and covered her all over with toothpaste. Now, let's all have some champagne."

Rosa did not like "hussies," as she called the unrichly dressed girls who made the mistake of coming into her front hall at the invitation of some never-to-be-forgiven guest. "Hussies," she would say, "I don't want hussies here." They would giggle embarrassedly and leave, the cheap furs around their necks jiggling, as in feigned disdain they turned to exit through the swinging doors.

But to be a lady at the Cavendish—ah, that was the place to let your hair down. And it was a lady who taught me that the chase could go the other way.

"The Lady Ann" I shall call her, because that was not her name and the important word in the title she bore was the article "the." Lady Jamison would have connoted marriage to a peer but "The Lady Ann" meant that the blood flowed direct.

And in this instance, strong. The Lady Ann took me by the hand (I think there was some pretext of carrying her bag to her room) and sat me down in front of one of those blue-flamed gas fireplaces with which the old Cavendish was equipped. Leaving me there for a moment, she retired to another place and when I heard the words, "Take your clothes off, please," I looked up from my chair astonished to see that she had removed all of her own.

The Lady Ann was an extremely good-looking girl, tall, slim, black hair tumbling to the shoulders with good legs and a well-proportioned figure. She stood there before me, confident, unembarrassed and strong. I wish memory afforded me a similar assessment of myself. Alas, I was frightened, embarrassed, awkward and ashamed. I rose, excused myself with a stammer, and fled.

Even now, there is something sad and painful about the memory of this episode. The feelings of guilt at the time, and the next morning when we encountered each other accidentally in the

Cavendish lobby, the questioning, not only of one's manhood, but of one's mores. Who taught me that it was I who must attack? Who told me that it was unmanly to be propositioned, unfeminine to propose?

Was it every novel I'd ever read—Hemingway, Dreiser, Lewis? Was it those four years at college among people who talked about "Wait until I get to Northampton"? Was it my sister with "her own" room? Was it all those silly politenesses—waiting for a girl to go in the door first, or out of the elevator first? Was it offering the seat on the bus? (I still do that because my mother told me I had to.) Was it years and years of getting out from behind a steering wheel, going around to the other side of the car and opening a door for a girl whose strength would surely not have been taxed if she had done it for herself?

I do not know the answers but my children will never have to ask the questions. Take Susan, for example, who likes a boy named Mark. Susan is a hiker and backpacker and hard tennis player, a fine short-stop and a left-handed passer. My friend Eddie Williams, who owns the Washington Redskins, says she's a very good left-handed passer. What he really says when he sees Susan throw a football is "My God!"

But Susan's relationship with Mark is one of casual equality. I don't know whether they sleep together. They might; they're very good friends. But if they do, I am certain that Mark does not attack. Attack is out now, along with show girls, striptease, pink lampshades and finishing schools.

Or take Mary, whom I noticed the other night swimming naked in the pool with two friends, both boys, both naked also. I could never have done it. Shyness would have overwhelmed me. Indeed, it overwhelmed me when I saw Mary. Tommy said, "Golly, that Mary—no pants," and I said, "What do you mean?" And Tommy gestured toward the pool and there she was, and there they were. But I resisted an impulse to shout my protest across the yard.

What harm was being done? If they were unselfconscious, why should I embarrass them? Only, as I say, I never could have done it when I was her age. The serpent which brought shame to Adam and Eve, causing them to don clothing, passed that shame through all the generations unto me and then suddenly, the serpent's will did not work any more. This generation dwells in the pre-serpent garden of Eden, and it must be a very pleasant place to dwell.

No guilt. No shame. No worry. No calling up parents to say "it" might have happened. Sex is not only free but, as far as I can see, grounded in total equality.

How easy it is. No role of the proposer for the boy; no role of the consenter for the girl; no chase; no attack. Just easy.

But I have worried about Elizabeth, Tommy and Nicky, the three youngest children, who don't know anything about sex and whose ignorance I have some possibly illogical desire to preserve. I tell myself that it's wrong for them to see boys freely entering their sisters' bedrooms. And then

I argue with myself: "It's all so natural. They're listening to records." And then I argue back: "What if the records are just a cover for something else?" And again, "Well, what if they are?" So what should I do? Bang on the bedroom door and say, "What are you doing in there?"

I tried a compromise. No boys upstairs at night. I don't know why that rule seemed to bridge the time gap between the old and the new. Or avoid the issue I was posing to myself by its suggestion that with the younger children asleep in their rooms, record playing should be prohibited at night. But it did. And it works, more or less.

Except the other night Joan and I got home about eleven and coming up the stairs I ran into David's friend Patrick and his girl coming down. Patrick is an awfully nice Irish boy with an extremely winsome smile, and his girl, whom I call the painter, is very pretty and paints very well. Patrick smiled and said, "Hello, Mr. Braden." And I said, "Patrick, you two know you're not supposed to be upstairs at night." And then, by way of explanation, I added, "I've got eight-year-old kids up here." Patrick smiled again. "Mr. Braden," he said, "we're not interested in eight-year-old kids. We're only interested in each other."

It's Not My Fault

As I said, guilt about clothes I inherited from Adam and Eve. I like to wear clothes and am embarrassed when other people do not wear them.

Moreover, I find logic in this view beyond everyman's inheritance. My experience is that there are very few people who do not look better with their clothes on than with their clothes off. Clothes on, it is possible to imagine a well-formed person. But most people are not well formed. The old limerick

> Breasts and bosoms I have known
> Of various shapes and sizes
> From poignant disillusionment
> To jubilant surprises.

offers hope, but there are not really very many jubilant surprises. If there had been, streaking might have become an important institution instead of an overnight fad.

And yet the guilt overrules the logic, as I discovered that summer night when Joan and I came home to find all five girls standing around naked by the swimming pool. None of them are poignant disillusionments. All of them are very good-looking girls. The fact did not assuage my sense of shock.

"What in the world," I said, addressing Mary as the oldest, "are you doing?"

"We are," she said, "having a swim."

"No, no, no," I said. "That's not it. I mean what are you doing standing here naked? Someone might easily come through the gate and into the yard. Someone could see you from the street. Now, all of you," I continued, still addressing Mary, "get upstairs and put some clothes on."

And Mary looked back at me, coolly. "What's the matter with you, Dad?" she asked. "Do you feel guilty?"

The answer, obviously, is yes, I do. And afterward I asked myself, "How did I ever bring up five girls who think it's all right to stand out by the swimming pool in a suburban community without any clothes on?" Granted, it was dark. Granted, there is shrubbery. I still felt guilty.

There are other kinds of guilt, just as deep-seated and impossible to set aside. Why, for example, does Elizabeth tell stories? Why does she tell stories so guilelessly, with such innocence of appearance, such sweetness? If the stories she concocts were as good as her manner of telling them, it would be impossible ever to pin her down.

"Thank you for your note asking that Elizabeth

be excused from school next Wednesday," was the way the letter to Joan began, and since Joan had not written any such note, it was necessary to confront Elizabeth. Elizabeth said it must have been a mistake on the part of the school. She would find out.

When you have eight children, it is impossible to do all the little chores you might do if you had one. I suppose that if Elizabeth had been an only child, Joan or I would have gone to the school, asked to see the note, and confronted Elizabeth with the forgery.

But there was enough to do. Tommy had to be driven to school that morning and so did Nicky, and Joan had an early appointment at the office. So we did not go out and collect the evidence. We waited.

Elizabeth had to be reminded of her promise about looking into it. And then she was ready with the following story: "Some of the kids wanted to try out the new principal, just to see how he'd act, you know. So they wrote him a letter excusing me from school and signed Mother's name to it."

A likely story. A story neither of us believed. We told Elizabeth we didn't believe it. But we did not take the trouble to prove the case to her. So I feel guilty about Elizabeth's stories and guilty that I have not converted the fault. How long will Elizabeth go on like this? Mary used to tell stories when she was younger, and she used to pocket things too. I remember the time I turned around at the restaurant to see if I'd left anything behind and there was Mary, a pretty little girl of nine in a blue dress, looking sweet and pocketing the tip I had left for the waitress. She doesn't tell stories or pocket any more. Maybe Elizabeth will grow out of it too. I tell myself so. And yet I avoided the embarrassing confrontation, and so I go on feeling guilty. I hate confrontations because they usually leave me feeling guilty too. There I was, sitting on the back porch and not paying much attention and Joan was telling Nancy she couldn't spend a weekend on a motorcycle with her love affair. And suddenly I heard Nancy shout at her mother, making frequent use of a four-letter word. So there I was with a confrontation. Anger rose, I struck Nancy. Doubtless she deserved it. Nevertheless, I felt guilty for days. Now that I recall the incident, I still do.

The only way I know to avoid guilt is to pay no attention. Go about your own business and tell yourself, when suspicion dawns, that it's better not to know. But then ugly fact is forced upon you—the fender of the car is dented, the dollar you put in your desk drawer is not there. The suspicion you felt at the time was justified and you should have done something about it when you felt suspicion and not waited until when there has to be a confrontation. Guilt again.

When you think about your children, guilt runs deep. The time you didn't spend; the toys you should have bought instead of those you did buy; the tennis court you could never afford; the music lessons not given; the dancing classes ignored, and ignored despite your knowledge that Elizabeth wanted to go to them, and is naturally an extremely graceful girl, and acrobatic as well. All those other talents and interests you forgot to push, or didn't have time to push, or money to push with.

And the moments which may have been or may turn out to be crucial—moments when courses in college were chosen and you promised to consult and didn't. Why is Nicky the only child in the family who can't really swim, who never learned to make a stroke but only how to duck and tumble in the waves? Because you never taught him to swim, that's why. You taught all the others and ignored Nicky because you were too busy at the time when Nicky should have learned to swim.

And if you didn't spend enough time, you spent too much time. Why did it take David so long to go to college? And why is he so diffident about it? Because you pushed college at him so hard and so often and with such vigor that college began to terrify him, that's why, and if he never gets an education, it's your fault.

"It's your fault," is a sentence frequently used in a house containing eight children. It is used when the milk gets spilled and the glass gets broken and the lawn mower is left out in the rain and the shoes are lost and the phonograph records are left on the floor and the car is damaged. My son, Nicholas, at nine, has developed a defensive statement of the facts as he sees them. He goes about all day, repeating to himself, in singsong manner, "It's not my fault; it's not my fault; not my fault." Nicholas emphasizes first the word "my" and then the word "fault," as though he were trying out in his mind which manner of saying the sentence "It's not my fault" rings the more solidly or gives him the greater satisfaction.

It occurred to me the other day that maybe there is logic and peace of mind in Nicholas' discovery. Joan and I were talking about Nancy and the love affair and David and college and we were feeling guilty as usual and asking each other what ought to be done, and suddenly Nicholas' favorite sentence came to mind. And I said to myself, why not? I have, I said to myself, provided a roof and meals and a place to play. I have provided schooling. I have provided advice. I have provided transportation. I have provided books. I have provided vacations. If I skipped the tennis lessons, I nevertheless provided riding lessons; silly, maybe, but that's what they said they wanted. I skipped some other things. But I did the best I could. Not the best of all possible worlds, but the best I could do.

So if somebody doesn't want to go to college; if somebody insists on a silly and premature love affair; if somebody is not going to turn out the way I think he or she would like himself to turn out; if, indeed, every one of them wants to say "The hell with it—I won't do what I'm supposed to do," and it all ends badly and someday I wake up to news that one of them is in jail, and I ought to be ashamed, you know what I'll do? I won't feel guilty. I'll imitate Nicholas. I'll go around saying to myself, "It's not my fault."

I said that to Joan and it sounded pretty good when I said it. "Damned if I'll ever feel guilty," I said. But, of course, I know I will.

The Go-Girl

Once upon a time there was a girl who did everything right and was not a goody-goody. She was good looking but never had to run the dangers of being thought beautiful. She was a good athlete but not a tomboy; a good student but not a grind; responsible but to common sense; not a stickler for rules; brave but accustomed to fear. In everything she did, she made an effort and therefore everything she did she enjoyed doing.

This girl was named Susan and I wonder what happens to such girls. Do they marry a John Adams, like Abigail, and influence history in ways which scholars eventually discern? Are they the unknown stalwarts who, according to the Talmud, uplift the world on their shoulders? Are they the Sarahs of the world like the one in the Bible who was remembered because she was cheerful?

Or does the world eventually twist these Susans who greet it so fully and with such steadfast mien, misshaping their spirit, poisoning them with such meanness and cruelty as the world can bestow?

I ask the question because experience tells me that there are more Susans at fourteen than there are at thirty and more at thirty than at fifty. Something must happen to them along the way, some accident, some husband, some bottle of gin. And sometimes, of course, they get through. We all know a few Susans, but not, I think, very many.

In the meantime, however, it is very pleasant to sit back and enjoy them. What is Susan doing now? She is playing hard tennis; she is speaking Spanish; she is waterskiing; she is playing second base on a team in which the other positions are played by eight boys; she is out running the mile; she is correcting her father's temper, saying, "Dad, you're being ridiculous"; she is reading history; she has gone to Mexico.

It doesn't matter what she is doing because if Susan is doing something, it is worth doing and she is doing it well and cheerfully, and with enough effort to learn from doing it. Or, if she is going somewhere, she is going responsibly and gracefully, taking pleasure in the going and she will get back when she says she will.

I worry about Mary, Nancy and Elizabeth being out late for many reasons. I worry about Joannie being out late because Joannie is so little and so sweet and so kind that she stirs up my protective instincts and I fear she may have met some circumstance she cannot overcome and that I ought to go at once and help. I never worry about Susan being out late because it gives me pleasure to think that she must be having a good time.

People say—Nancy sometimes says—"Susan is Dad's favorite." It is not true. I have no favorites. What is true is that I hardly ever disapprove of Susan, and the reason for that is that she seldom does anything to deserve it. Nor is she the object of jealousy from her brothers and sisters. It is hard to be jealous of somebody who is always up and doing. Logic says, "If I am jealous, why don't I be up and doing myself?" Or, as Joannie put it, "God, that Susan!"

I wish I were equally sure of the reason for Susan. Why do not all people know that the fun is in the trying?

"You ought to tell her not to apply to Dartmouth," a friend told me. "Her SAT's are very low, and she'll never make it." So I broached the subject. "I'm not worried, Dad," said Susan. "Those Dartmouth guys think they're such big shots. I can do anything they can." "All right," I said, "but what if you don't make it?" "Then I'll do something else," she answered. "And the only thing I'd be sorry about is that I didn't have a chance to try."

So she applied and was rejected and she took it pretty well but I knew she was hurt. "Those damned SAT's." I felt that way, too. I hate SAT's. First Mary, then Joannie, then Susan had gone through high school, often to more than one high school, getting good grades—A's and B's, and mostly A's—and then gone off to some testing center to be rated as a dummy by the SAT's.

Seven-hundred scores is what colleges look for

in the SAT, or six hundred at the least, and my children were coming home with scores in the five-hundred range and in tears. I remember standing out in front of the house one day, picking some weeds out of the pachysandra and the car came up and Joannie got out, running into the house as fast as she could and she was crying uncontrollably. I caught up with her and held her tight and tried to get her to stop and all she could sob out was "I can't, Dad. I can't. I try and try and I can't." Joannie took SAT's three times and three times she failed. And Nancy. The best grades in the family. Straight A's right through high school. Top of the class. Low SAT's. I think the SAT's are responsible for Nancy's decision to stay out of college and go off to Alaska with the love affair. Oh, I know the testers who make up the SAT would not say she failed. But for a child with good grades and ambitions for college, a score in the four hundreds or low five hundreds is a failure and I think I do not exaggerate when I say it must blight some of them for life. For it says to them at a very early age, "There is not much point in your trying. You are not very bright."

And I'm not sure that's true. Professor Banish Hoffman in his book *The Tyranny of Testing* says it isn't. The really bright student, he says, does poorly on the SAT's because the really bright student is stumped by the ambiguity of the multiple choice questions. He knows too much. I like some of Hoffman's examples of this ambiguity: "George Washington was born on February 22,

1732. True. False." As Professor Hoffman points out, anyone with a superficial knowledge of George Washington will say that the statement is true and "true" is the correct answer. But anyone with more than superficial knowledge might choose "false" as the answer because anyone with more than superficial knowledge knows that Washington was born under the Julian calendar, which reckoned that the date of his birth was February 11.

Or again, Hoffman points to the following test question: " 'Emperor' is the name of: (A) a string quartet; (B) a piano concerto; (C) a violin sonata." An average student answers (B) because an average student knows about Beethoven's piano concerto. But more well-informed students are stumped. They know about Beethoven's concerto but they also know about Haydn's quartet. So they wonder: Did the man who wrote the question know too?

But my favorite question among those which Dr. Hoffman uses is about the wind. It is my favorite because it seems to me totally ambiguous and I would have no way of deciding which answer was right and which wrong: "If we cannot make the wind blow when and where we wish it to blow, we can at least make use of its: (A) source; (B) heat; (C) direction; (D) force; (E) atmosphere." The correct answer is (D) but I do not see why a student shouldn't with equal logic choose (C), and Hoffman points out that a scientifically minded student who knows that "source of the wind" implies the combination of the heat of the sun and the rotation of the earth might well choose (A).

I don't say my children are really bright students. But Mary got A's and B's in high school, a mediocre SAT score and A's and B's in college.

I have talked to college admissions officers about this correlation and they all tell me that, of course, SAT's don't measure effort or initiative or patience or determination. They admit too that SAT's can't measure a person's ability to express himself clearly or forcefully or gracefully or even to reason excellently. An incorrect conclusion, Hoffman points out, arrived at by excellent argument, often has greater merit than a correct conclusion arrived at by appalling illogic or simple memorization of the professor's lecture. SAT's take no account of this truth.

But, the college admissions officers say, they only use SAT's as "one factor" in determining college admissions. The letter from Dartmouth that Susan got said that too. But it said that in this instance, the one factor was determining because the average SAT scores of Dartmouth's entering class would be in the high six hundreds and Susan's middle five hundred was "out of range."

There wasn't anything I could do about it, I explained to Susan. "If it were some other college," I told her, "I'd try. But Dartmouth is special to me. I went there. I'm on the board there. The man who wrote you that letter is an old and valued friend. This is the one time and in the one place where I can't help."

Susan understood. My wife did not. Joan arched her back like a mother cat whose kittens are under siege. I was to go to Dartmouth's President Kemeny, Joan said. I was to insist that a mistake had been made. "I can't," I explained. "You are asking me to go over the head of an old friend who has made a decision he thinks is correct and which he very much wishes he didn't have to make, and you want me to tell his boss that he is wrong. I can't do that." "Tom Braden," Joan replied, "you are wrong." "No," I answered, "I am not wrong. There are some things you can't do for your own children and this is one of them."

And so we left it. And one afternoon while Dartmouth's trustees were seated around their table discussing affairs of moment to the college, Joan walked into the office of President John Kemeny and left a note of moment to Susan.

I didn't know about it at the time and when I discovered what my wife had done I was embarrassed. I called my friend, the admissions officer, and I apologized. I felt guilty the next time I saw Dartmouth's president. I thought maybe the other trustees were looking upon me as one who had let down the side. Honorable men, all of them. I was sure they would not have taken advantage of their position. Moreover, I remarked to Joan, I was sure they had greater control over their wives.

I felt these things deeply, so much so that I found myself skipping the next trustees' meeting. I would have felt as though they were all looking at me.

Moreover, as Kemeny pointed out to Joan—or so she told me—what Joan did might be harmful to Susan. Not being admitted was a painful blow but flunking out would be more painful. He had wanted Joan to understand the implications of the decision she was making. If she was willing to accept those implications, he was willing to reconsider.

So I worried about the implications and I worried about what Joan had done and I worried about my friend, the admissions officer, and my relationship with him, and I worried about the fact that the whole episode left me feeling guilty. And then Susan's first grades arrived in the mail one morning and there it was again—A's and B's.

Maybe another thing that SAT's don't measure is whether the girl who takes them also takes the advice of her father—as Susan does. I don't mean on the tests, but in general. I told Susan she was a fool if she started to smoke. I told Susan she'd be better off to read a good book or improve her tennis than to hang around during the summer with a gang whose object appears to be to hang around. I told Susan that the great mistake most people made in all of life was not to try. I've told all the rest of my girls these things too, but they don't pay quite so much attention.

Every morning during the decade of the sixties I got up in our Oceanside house and went down the steps and ran a mile along the beach. And one morning, I looked back a couple of hundred yards and there was a trim six-year-old racing along behind me. We kept that up, Susan and I, for years, and sometimes others came along, Nancy particularly, but not every single morning, rain or shine, summer or winter, as Susan did.

After a while, Susan was no longer catching up with me, but I was working hard, ploughing through sand, trying to stay in step with her. I reminded her of that fact not long ago and she laughed and said, "Go, Dad. Go."

That's the way it is with Susan.

Help

My friend Joseph Alsop says that "help" is a nice-nelly word and refuses to use it. "Servant," Joe says, "is accurate and objective, while 'help' is not quite accurate because it is subjective, indicating the obeisance of him who is served to the great god of egalitarianism."

Joe may be right for himself. He is wrong for me. I have hired a lot of people over the years to help Joan and me bring up eight children. Some of them have helped and some of them have hindered. But by none have I ever felt served.

I don't mean that I haven't been grateful. I think for example of Beatrice. Beatrice was born on a Maryland farm and she is still a country girl at heart, honest and open and trusting. I am sure she thinks of herself also as help and not as a servant. And, perhaps partly as a result of how she thinks of herself, Beatrice is a friend who has been steady as a rock in times of crisis and is always reliable, always there.

I pay Beatrice, and pay her pretty well and I should, because she comes in every morning surely and leaves late. But throughout many long days, I don't remember Joan and me ever giving her an "order." In our family we cope and Beatrice knows we are coping and she helps and we are grateful.

Beatrice and I are the joint keepers of the keys, that is, we both have a set and she lends me hers when I have mislaid mine. Therefore, we are both authority figures. Our keys unlock the liquor closet, the laundry room, and a small room in the kitchen in which I presume some former owner of our old house sheltered his fine silver. Beatrice uses it to shelter anything that is impossible to preserve in the open.

Thus, Beatrice's closet hides Triscuits, cigarettes, vases, the good napkins, a spare corkscrew and peanut butter.

The Triscuits are for Joan, who likes them and could never have them if they were put in the kitchen because the children, who don't really care what they eat after school so long as they eat, would wipe them out daily. The cigarettes and good napkins are also hidden against children, particularly Elizabeth, who pretends she doesn't smoke, and against Tommy, who has used good napkins to clean up dog messes. The spare corkscrew is for me and is hidden against guests of the children who bring in bottles of wine, consume them in upstairs rooms, and ditch the bottle and the corkscrew under the bed.

The vases are hidden against the wagging tails of dogs, and the spare peanut butter means there is only one jar of peanut butter in the kitchen at any one time, whereas, if there were two or three, the children—for some reason I have never fathomed—would open them all.

I know a man who has three well-behaved and well-cared-for children and who has said of me and of my family, "Those Bradens are gypsies." His remark was reported to me, and the reporter, I think, was surprised that I took no offense whatever. I think the description is accurate, and Beatrice's closet helps to prove it. It contains the gypsy hoard.

The laundry room is also locked, not in order to hoard clothing but to preserve the machinery, and to try to bring some order to the washing and ironing of clothes. We got along all right with an unlocked laundry room until the children were able to wash their own blue jeans. You'd think this stage might be a welcome one to a large family, but it is not so. As everybody knows, the thing to do with a new pair of blue jeans is not to wear them but to wash them—a hundred times and more—before you think of putting them on. "That washing machine is gone already," Beatrice reported one day in September, speaking of a washing machine we had acquired the previous Christmas. "It's been done in by overalls." When the children washed their blue jeans, the clothes which Beatrice was washing were put aside by each successive blue-jean washer and successive blue-jean washers usually left the dryer on too, with a pair of tennis shoes bouncing around inside.

So I went to the laundry room, and stared at the broken machine with the blue jeans inside it and looked about me at the disheveled piles of children's clothing, and I said, "Ye, Gods" and Beatrice said, "These children."

So, with my permission, Beatrice had a lock put on the laundry room door, and out of a sense of conspiracy and secret sharing, she had a key made for me too, although I never use it, and have not visited the laundry room since that day on which I looked and said, "Ye Gods."

The reason I mention the locked closets and the keys is that they are the subject of considerable resentment among the children, who argue that it deprives them of basic rights, like being able to get another jar of peanut butter when the old one is out, or wash a pair of blue jeans which have not been washed sufficiently to be worn without embarrassment.

"There's something wrong about a house with locked doors," David remarked the other day. I think he does not understand that the locked doors are essential to keeping Beatrice as a helper. In my opinion, if there is one thing worse than a house with locked doors, it is a house with eight children and no help.

Up to three children, I think Joan and I could have managed. After that, never.

We have had over the years a considerable parade of "help," though it has been nothing like those stories I used to hear of the Robert Kennedy family—one maid arriving and another leaving every other day or week. But as memory now casts the faces of "help" before me in sequence, I count fourteen, and I am including Pablo and his wife from El Salvador.

Pablo believed that his wife should labor long and that he should watch, which was the way—or so he said—that they did things "in my country." He explained about "my country" frequently, but I still could not accustom myself to the sight of Pablo's wife, down on her hands and knees, scrubbing the kitchen floor, while Pablo looked on approvingly. I would get down on my hands and knees and take the brush away from her and scrub the floor in front of Pablo, and I thought it might shame him. But since he had already explained to me how things went in "my country," he assumed, I suppose logically, that this demonstration on my part showed a dissatisfaction with his wife's labor. So Pablo left, taking his servant with him.

Not counting Pablo, the average length of time in which real "help" has helped has been about two years, and I'm rather proud, now that I think of it, to note that all of them were friends and many of them still are.

Joe Alsop's point is that since Americans consider it degrading to be servants, they have made use of the noun "help" in order to disguise the fact that they find servants indispensable. But I doubt that Joe has ever examined the difference between help and servants. Servants serve meals. Help helps serve meals. Servants make beds and clean up bathrooms. Help helps make sure the children do it. Servants wait upon others. In our house, others often wait upon the help.

So, the word "help" in our country has become nearly synonomous with the word "hand," as my father used to say. The hand on the Kansas farm of my grandfather was often a young fellow working to get his own piece of land and quite eligible to squire my father's sisters to the village dance on a Saturday night.

"Help" in the middle-class home of today is likely to be female but except for that distinction, the job has much the same stature as that of the "hand." Help—except upon occasions of company for dinner—eats at the same table, takes possession of a good room and a television set—if "help" decides to "live in"—has Sundays and every other Saturday off, and is consulted about every family problem from meals and report cards to vacation journeys and the purchase of refrigerators and cars.

Moreover, help is granted a certain immunity from criticism and quarrelsomeness. It is all right— at least it is all right at our house—for a child to say his mother or father at dinner that she or he is talking nonsense, but it is not all right to say the same to Beatrice.

There have been mistakes, of course. We have employed as help one alcoholic and two nymphomaniacs.

The alcoholic was very secretive about her problem and disguised it so well with mouthwash that it was not until after she left that we discovered her weakness. Joan and I had to get boxes from the grocery store to hold all the empty bottles secreted behind her closet door.

I learned about one of the nymphomaniacs from the Oceanside police, whose curiosity had been aroused by the sudden popularity of our hitherto quiet and attractionless street to squadrons of Marine Corps recruits from nearby Camp Pendleton. The other I learned about from my small daughters, who were learning things during the night time which astonished me when they were related in the day.

When I think back upon the alcoholic and the nymphomaniacs, I am sorry. We should have known better and spared our children. Nevertheless, I shrug my shoulders. What would Joan and I have done if there had been no help at all?

If you estimate that each child goes through ten diapers a day for two years, that's seven thousand and three hundred diaper changes, and for eight children it comes to a grand total of fifty-eight thousand, four hundred.

Or take meals. The average age of the children now is sixteen. If my arithmetic is right, that means that Joan and I and the help have served them roughly one hundred and forty thousand, one hundred and sixty meals—and washed the dishes and put them away—though, of course, the children helped as they grew older.

Servants don't know how to help. I think for example of Sing, a Chinese man, who came to us from Hong Kong and was in every respect a servant.

Everybody in the family liked Sing. He was

cheerful. He was enormously efficient. He cooked excellent Chinese meals and cleaned the house better than it was cleaned before or has been cleaned since.

Moreover, he took his job as servant in the very ancient sense, as a vassal and protector. We kept a surfboard outside the Oceanside house and the neighborhood teen-age boys were accustomed to borrowing it. One day I looked out the window and saw two boys lugging the surfboard up the steep bank to its customary place outside the back door. Ten feet behind them, in silent pursuit, was Sing, bearing in an outstretched hand a great kitchen knife, by the show of which, he had forced them to return what he thought was stolen property.

But the trouble with Sing was that he insisted on doing things himself, and it was obvious to me that eventually he would explode. Anyone who tries to be a servant in a house of eight children will explode.

Sing's explosion was gentle. He insisted that none of the eight children could ever enter the kitchen and that he would serve them, outside the kitchen. This was a reasonable demand for a servant to make. But it was not a demand which "help" would ever make because help understands democracy and democracy begins in the kitchen. Children home from school want a glass of milk and a peanut butter sandwich. They should get it for themselves and clean up afterward. What red-blooded American boy or girl wants a peanut butter and jelly sandwich served on a plate? I

liked Sing and I was sorry to see him go, but as
I think back now on the differences between the
servant and the help, I think of Sing on the one
hand and on the other, my mind conjures up the
enormous figure of a man named Dick.

Dick was a buck sergeant in the Marine Corps,
who came to stay with us because his wife, Louise,
a beautiful woman, was "help." Dick wasn't paid.
He just lived with us once in a while and did
special jobs in repayment for room and board.
Dick had a disability pension for some ailment
he must have overcome. For he was well over
two hundred pounds of muscle. He could lift a
car off the ground by its rear axle. He could eat
enormous quantities of food—whole chickens
would disappear down his gold-edged mouth in
a single sitting. And he handled a horse as though
it were an undersized child.

Dick's stint as "help" in our family lasted
throughout a love affair he had with a barrel
racer named "Lady Golden," whom Dick met one
summer while we were vacationing in Aspen,
Colorado. Until he saw Lady Golden win a local
barrel race, Dick never showed any interest in
horses. But after that race, he talked of nothing
else and he hung around Lady Golden's stall,
caressing her and talking to her and telling her
what a fine barrel racer she was.

I guess she was, too. I saw her once or twice in
a race, and the turn she executed, in which, after
going full speed at the barrel at one end of the
course, skidding to a virtual halt when she reached
it, lunging around it on her knees, and then charg-

ing back again full tilt at the barrel on the other end of the course, was spectacular.

Indeed, Lady Golden was a powerful quarter horse, of a color her name aptly described, and with a white mane hung down over her eyes which she tossed from side to side in defiance. She was free spirited, this horse, unaccustomed to greater discipline than that which could be enforced by a hackamore and dubious about whether she would accept even that.

Lady Golden appealed to Dick so greatly that when it came time to pack up the car and go back to Oceanside, he bought her. I was informed of the purchase just the day before departure, I supposed because I was driving the station wagon and Dick knew it would be necessary to attach a trailer to its rear end.

But I found there was an additional reason. The purchase price of Lady Golden had put Dick out of funds and he asked me whether, as a favor to him, I would buy the trailer.

So Dick and I hunted around Aspen and found an old horse trailer without a top and I bought it for fifty dollars and we got Lady Golden into it and set out for home, not deviating from our planned route, which included—Joan had arranged it—a detour through Bryce Canyon National Park.

One of the things which is notable about Bryce Canyon National Park is the series of natural bridges and tunnels through which the road winds. Many people, driving across country or through the West, are thrilled by these monuments and, as is well known, children enjoy them because the moment the car enters they can raise their voices and hear them echo against the rock walls.

But to this day, I think of the tunnels of Bryce Canyon with a dread which approaches fear. For Lady Golden, riding in her open trailer, saw each tunnel coming and let forth a whinny of such power and treble that as the sound bounced back and forth between the tunnel walls, it became truly terrifying, and totally encompassing, ruling out speech, thought, decision, even identity.

Other motorists were petrified. They pulled over sharply to the side of the tunnel and stopped, which is dangerous and against the law. If it had not been for the massive rock of the tunnels, they would unquestionably have plunged off the road. My own fear should have been tempered after a time by experience, but somehow as we approached each tunnel, the knowledge of what was to come served me as the sight of an instrument of torture is said to serve the man who has felt its pain.

Fortunately, the Bryce Canyon drive is short, and we were out of the park and in the clear before travelers in the opposite direction could report the disturbances, before park officials could intervene, and before we met that driver, whom the law of averages suggests would plunge *at* us instead of away.

Throughout all this, Dick, in the back seat, murmured reassurance. "The Lady will be all right," he would say, in the tone of a man spreading ointment on a sore. Once through the tunnels, she was.

I had not realized that so many towns in this country keep a stable as a municipal service to the traveler who wishes to put his horse up for the night. I doubt that many of the inhabitants of our towns realize it either. I don't know what I thought we were going to do with Lady Golden when we stopped during the thousand-mile trip from Colorado to California. Did I suppose that Dick and I would walk her around while she nibbled on the lawn outside the motel where the children slept?

I have an impression now of grizzled old men, some in boots and cowboy hats, some in ordinary overalls, who keep the town stable, and without having to go beyond the first policeman we encountered, we found it, unhooked the trailer from the station wagon full of children, and quartered Lady Golden for the night.

The difficulty was the morning after, when Dick and I would arrive to load Lady Golden for the next stage in the journey. At all the stops, the grizzled stablemen agreed: "She's a good looker but she won't load." Lady Golden balked and kicked and we would strain and push and get her halfway up the ramp onto the trailer, when she would rear onto her hind legs, and the stablemen and Dick and I would lose our grips or our courage and she would come off the ramp again.

As it turned out, it was all very much worthwhile. Lady Golden was a great joy to Dick and to us. Dick and David took first prize in an Oceanside parade one Labor Day, with David riding

Lady Golden as Huckleberry Finn, and Dick walking alongside as Jim. The following year Dick caparisoned Lady Golden with a great silver-plated saddle and silver-plated fittings which hung down all around, so that she gleamed in the sunlight. Then he rode her down Oceanside's Main Street, not for any prize at all, but simply to take part in the parade.

The whole family stood together and cheered and clapped as Dick rode by. He was too big really for Lady Golden; his feet nearly touched the ground. But he was proud and beautiful all the same.

I don't know where Dick and Louise are now, but whenever I think of "help" and also about important moments of pride and triumph in our family, I think of Dick on Lady Golden, riding down Oceanside's Main Street, in the parade.

Mrs. Clark Goes to Africa

I put Joan on the plane to Africa one bright afternoon in June, and it wasn't until several days later that I realized Mrs. Clark had gone too.

It always works that way. I mean, it's Joan that's going, dressed and packed, and with a book under her arm, feeling very sentimental and looking very little-girl-like. "Tom," she said, in a frightened, small voice as we approached the gate, and she turned her face up to kiss me goodbye, "I'm really going now; I'm really going to Africa."

There was a Peace Corps type, a casual acquaintance, and like Joan, employed by a worthy organization called Save the Children Federation who was taking the same plane. He looked at her, crisp and scrubbed and beautiful in the neat white khaki bush jacket with the black buttons. "Yes," he said, "and obviously for the first time."

And so Joan left. But it was Mrs. Clark who turned out a couple of days later to be gone. Joan is a little girl with a perpetual tan who dresses for the occasion, loves parties and people and loves, most of all, as she puts it, "to get to go."

Mrs. Clark, on the other hand, has little time for such nonsense. Mrs. Clark sees that each child has something to do; she plans next steps about problems with each child in turn. Mrs. Clark loves each and all together. She arranges family vacations and outings. She likes boys with haircuts and eventually prevails; she doesn't believe in failure on the part of any member of her family; yet she is understanding, wise, comforting, shrewd and full of good advice about any member's temporary defeat.

As I say, whereas Joan is a little girl, Mrs. Clark is a sensible, grown-up woman. I love Joan a lot, but when she went to Africa, I missed Mrs. Clark the more.

"Mrs. Clark" was originally Tommy's name for his mother but it caught on because everyone realized that Tommy had defined the two-sidedness of Joan.

"Mom," Tommy would say, "can I go to the movies?" Permission to go to the movies is a minor problem. But take a serious problem. Take a problem such as wanting to change schools or go out for the basketball team and thus not be home three nights a week in time for dinner. "Mrs. Clark," Tommy will say on such occasions, "Mrs. Clark, I'd like to talk to you."

Talking with Mrs. Clark is always worthwhile. She is full of wise saws and modern instances. Also, she has many confidences which she will share, and these confidences bring out confidences in return, so that Mrs. Clark knows much more about the secret fears and desires, troubles and happinesses of my children than I do, and her advice to them comes from the understanding which mutual confidences bring.

Mrs. Clark is also the CIA of the family. At our house, if you want to get money from Dad, you have to confront him directly, state your case, be prepared to argue it, and to take the money openly, perhaps in front of others. It is, in effect, a grant, publicly stated as such and likely to be mentioned at the dinner table.

But Mrs. Clark, knowing as she does about secret troubles and difficulties which ought not to be mentioned aloud, will often fund covertly, as they say in the intelligence trade, using un-vouchered funds for the purpose, requiring no public accounting, and never to be mentioned again, "even to Dad."

Mrs. Clark is also a very brave woman. She thinks nothing of putting eight children in a station wagon and setting out across the country or taking off for India with the wife of the President of the United States because the President tells her at dinner one night that, of course, she can get the trip paid for by writing an article in "one of the magazines."

Sometimes Mrs. Clark's enormous self-confidence breaks down and then she calls me from some near or far-off place and becomes, quite suddenly, Joan again. Joan is dependent upon me; therefore, I feel superior. But Mrs. Clark assumes a co-equal status. Does some need to prove myself superior to Mrs. Clark, too, evoke the memory of an instance in which metamorphosis took place quite suddenly?

One one of the trips across the country with six of the eight, the drive shaft broke on the station wagon and Mrs. Clark hiked eleven miles in the Utah desert before she could find a telephone. Eleven miles in the hot sun had turned Mrs. Clark into Joan, and very nearly in tears.

I recall another telephone call, also the culmination of an adventure, but one in which the metamorphosis went the other way. The adventure itself had involved metamorphosis too.

It was Joan who agreed with President Kennedy one night at a White House dinner party that it would be fun to go to India with Jackie, but it was Mrs. Clark who arranged with Stewart Alsop to get the *Saturday Evening Post* to pay for the trip. It was Mrs. Clark who told Alsop that, of course, she would write an article for the *Post* about the trip just the moment she got back.

But it was Joan on the telephone from the American Embassy in London at seven one morning as I was getting out of bed in California. The voice was desperate. "The trip is over. We're leaving for Washington in about six hours. And I haven't anything to write. I can't just rewrite the pieces I've been sending home for the newspaper. It would be a list of palaces visited."

"Talk to Jackie," I advised.

"I haven't," she confessed, "seen Jackie since the first day, except at a distance."

I saw the problem. I had read the newspaper. Jackie visiting a palace with Nehru; Jackie visiting a monument with Nehru's daughter, Indira Gandhi; Jackie and her sister, Lee Radziwill, being entertained at a garden party; Jackie and Lee riding an elephant—all glimpsed and reported at respectful and secure distance by a dusty, sweating horde of "press."

A serious foreign affairs reporter who had been along on the trip told me later that from the standpoint of serious reporting, it was a disaster. By accident this serious foreign affairs reporter had once come within earshot of Mrs. Kennedy and Prime Minister Nehru. The secret service noted his presence and hustled him back to the press fold, where his friends gathered around demanding to know about his experience close up and what words he had heard.

"Nehru said the monument was fourteenth century," he confided. "And what," his comrades asked, "did Jackie say?" "I leaned forward," he related, "cupped my hands to the side of my mouth and whispered to the crowd: 'Jackie said, "Oh." ' "

I felt sorry for Joan. She had come down from the giddy heights of a White House dinner party and a talk with John F. Kennedy to the back of a press plane; from the status of press notice as "a friend of Mrs. Kennedy who is accompanying her" to being a reporter with dusty shoes and a dirty dress; from the excitement of having the *Saturday Evening Post* pay for a trip to India, to the flattening realization that she had nothing to say about the trip that hadn't been wire copy three weeks ago.

I thought of those pictures she had sent home by airmail; rolls of film from a camera she had borrowed from our newspaper. Small newspapers don't have cameras with telescopic lenses. But Joan had taken pictures nevertheless at every stop that Mrs. Kennedy made, and the professionals in the press, so she had written me, had felt sorry for her with her unprofessional camera, and had permitted her to get right up in front.

We had developed the pictures at the office. If we had possessed a powerful glass, and had held it to the print, we might have been able to satisfy ourselves that those tiny figures way off in the distance, through the iron bars which usually dominated the foreground, were the Prime Minister of India and the wife of the President of the United States. But as photographs for the newspaper, they were useless.

Joan had worked so hard to get those pictures. And she had been so excited to "get to go." Suddenly, I felt sad and wounded. "I don't know," I said. "Honestly, Joan, I don't know what to tell you to do."

It may be that the pathetic quality of my response and my admission of impotence regenerated that spark in my wife which Tommy defines as Mrs. Clark.

In any event, her voice immediately took on a firmer tone. "There's one thing I could do," she said. "I could write a note to Jackie and explain the problem and then get David to deliver it."

"David?" I asked. "David who?"

"David Bruce," she said.

Now, David Bruce was our ambassador to England. I knew him more or less in the fashion that a plain citizen may know his senator or a parts mechanic at the neighborhood service station may know the president of General Motors. During the war Mr. Bruce had been Colonel Bruce, second in command of the OSS, and so I could say that I had served under him, though he was not conscious of the fact. After the war, he had been a chief in the Marshall Plan and an ambassador to France, to England and to Germany, and I had worked with him—far down the line.

So I knew him—in fact, I had stayed one night at his residence in Paris and breakfasted with him in the morning. I admired him. I liked him. But I would no more have thought of asking him to deliver a note for me than I would have thought, back in the days of the war, of walking up to him, slapping him on the back and addressing him by his first name.

"If David delivered a note, Jackie would be sure to get it and sure to read it." Was that what Joan had said?

I demurred. "You can't ask him to do that," I replied.

But Mrs. Clark was now in full control. "Don't be silly," she said. "He won't mind at all. I'm sure he won't mind. That's exactly what I'll do."

And that was exactly what she did do. Perhaps Joan would have been able to deliver a note on her own. Perhaps Jackie would have seen a message so delivered. But it is certain that Ambassador Bruce was able to deliver the note and certain that Jackie saw it.

Joan and Jackie rode home on the plane together, seat by seat, and chatted about the trip, and Joan wrote everything down after they chatted. Back in Washington, the President himself went over the manuscript, inserting in his small, fine hand a suggestion with respect to Mrs. Kennedy's maid, Pruvie.

Alsop was amused when he saw the President's marginal note, "Say something nice about Pruvie," it read. "The dear old *Post*," Alsop remarked, "a chosen instrument for straightening out relations with the White House staff. Well, there are worse missions for men and magazines."

As I say, Mrs. Clark's own self-confidence occasionally cracks and when this occurs, Mrs. Clark simply ceases to be, and there is Joan again—tiny, vulnerable, and anxious to be cared for.

The times when Joan is going to be Joan and when she is going to be Mrs. Clark are fairly predictable. Any accident or external challenge to the family or any member thereof almost always brings Mrs. Clark to the fore. When the challenge has been met successfully, Mrs. Clark becomes Joan again.

The reason I needed Mrs. Clark during the summer that Joan went to Africa was the odd behavior of Mary. Joan had no sooner embarked upon her long journey than it was called to my attention that my oldest daughter was behaving, well, strangely.

"Where is Mary?" I asked as we sat down to dinner on the first night after Joan's departure.

"She's upstairs," Nicholas answered, "staring at the wall."

I raised an eyebrow toward Joannie, who replied, "That's literally true, Dad. Haven't you noticed? Mary is out of it."

We had a discussion about this at the table, quietly and somehow obliquely, and Joannie explained what she meant by "out of it."

"I mean if you say to Mary—it doesn't matter what you say to Mary—if you say, 'That happened during the Arab-Israeli war,' or you could say, 'I'm looking for the broom,' Mary will say nothing for a long time and then she will say, 'What do you mean, Arab-Israeli war? What was the Arab-Israeli war?' Or she will say, 'Broom? What do you mean, broom?' "

I confessed I had not noticed this behavior and I tended to disbelief. But the next day, driving downtown in the car with Mary on some joint errand, I was pulled up at a series of corners by red lights. "A lot of red lights," I remarked, vacuously, and Mary said nothing. And then, about two minutes later, she said, "Why, Dad? You think I am a red light?" Her voice was dull and expressionless. "Mary," I replied, "you'd better see a doctor." "Dad, I am seeing a doctor."

Three or four doctors, it turned out. Mary was apparently making the rounds of the city's psychiatrists, trying to decide which one she wanted, a fact I discovered that very afternoon, when one of them called to inquire why my daughter hadn't shown up for an appointment.

Mary was making a cry for help, I realized, and I was worried, and even a little frightened. I don't know anything about psychiatry or psychiatrists. But obviously, something was wrong. Mary explained that she was off to see another psychiatrist that afternoon. I decided to go along.

He seemed, this psychiatrist, much like any doctor of medicine, wearing the familiar white jacket of doctors, and very sure of himself. After he had talked privately to Mary for about ten minutes, he summoned me from the waiting room and came at once to the point.

"Your daughter," he said, "must enter a hospital at once. She is exhausted and on the verge of what you, as a layman, would call a 'nervous breakdown.'

"It may take a long time to find out the why of all this, Mr. Braden, but in the hospital we can begin to find out. I shall book a room this afternoon, and you should go now and pick up her things from home."

I gazed up at the diplomas on the wall. "Well," I said, "if you say so."

But Mary would not say so. Summoned from the waiting room for conference with both of us, she stood first before the doctor's desk, and then made a move toward the door. She had a hunted look on her face, and I thought for a moment she might flee. To the doctor she said, "I do not want to go to a hospital." Then turning to me, "Dad, why are you doing this to me? You know I don't want to go to a hospital. Dad,

I will not go to a hospital."

"I'm sure your father agrees with me," I heard the doctor saying.

"Mary," I responded, trying to be enthusiastic, "I could bring over that first volume of H. G. Wells you've been reading, and you could finish it in a couple of days. It might be fun—and restful —to get away from all your brothers and sisters."

"No, Dad. I will not go to a hospital."

The doctor motioned me to his inner office while Mary waited. "Look," he explained, after he had shut the door. "This might be very serious. Quite clearly, your daughter is not herself. You must get her to a hospital. I cannot otherwise be responsible."

I didn't know what he meant by being "otherwise responsible" but the words frightened me. For the first time I noticed his small, neatly trimmed mustache. It made him look more positive. I wished that I could talk to Mrs. Clark, who was by now, I reflected, in Upper Volta.

"I don't know," I said, "how I can get her to go to a hospital if she doesn't want to go to a hospital."

"Have you ever had a family conference, Mr. Braden?" he asked me. "If all her brothers and sisters tell her she would be wise to go to the hospital, wouldn't that help you? I've always found the family conference supportive."

"Maybe," I said, thinking about it. "I can try."

"Do. I think you'll find it supportive too."

Mary and I drove home in silence. Mary went immediately upstairs, and I went into my office, put my feet up on the table next to the typewriter and stared at the wall. Suddenly, the door to my office room burst open.

It was Elizabeth, her face pushed close to mine, her long red hair bobbing with fury, her blue eyes narrowed. "Dad, you're going to send Mary to a hospital? I'll tell you, Dad, you're not going to send Mary to a hospital. She'll run away before she lets you send her to a hospital, and I'll run away with her."

"Elizabeth," I said, removing my feet from the typewriter table, and standing against the assault, "you don't know anything about this. You don't know what the doctor said. You don't know what the dangers are. You haven't talked to me."

"I don't want to talk to you. I don't need to talk to you. I've talked to Mary." She burst out of the room, and out the front door, and I saw her heading down the street blindly, raging with the injustice of her father's cause.

Thus ended the notion of a family conference. I wondered what the doctor's family was like, and how he envisioned a family conference. Would there be a Bible? Would everybody remain silent until Father spoke? Would the children listen, wide-eyed, and nod sagely, as though he had expressed their very thought? Would they then suggest small, yet not insignificant ways in which they could aid Father's objective? And where was Mother? Sitting there with the knitting basket? Or in Upper Volta?

Again I thought of Mrs. Clark. Joan would not want Mary to go to a hospital. But Mrs. Clark might. On the other hand, Mrs. Clark might say, "Mary will come with me and we shall go off and lie on a beach somewhere and talk and then there will be no necessity for a hospital." Mrs. Clark might say, "She will recover because I shall see that she does."

But what was I to do without Mrs. Clark? I could not go off to the beach with Mary. I had a column to write, a television broadcast to perform. The doctor's warning was dread. How much did psychiatrists know?

I had no standard or experience by which to make a judgment. There were those diplomas on the wall. An M.D. at the University of Buffalo, psychiatry at Columbia. He must know more than I know. Perhaps, with Elizabeth out of the way, a family conference was possible still.

It was a Sunday afternoon. Nancy had, after all, gone off to Alaska with the love affair. David, Susan, Tommy and Nicky had gone fishing. I waited until they arrived and told David and Susan I wished to see them. Tommy and Nicky were at once suspicious. They hung near the door.

We sat down quietly in the office and I began the tale of the day's discovery. "Mary," I said, midway into the story, "has apparently been seeing a number of psychiatrists, seeing them once, making appointments for a second visit and then not going back." I was about to explain that this knowledge had persuaded me to accompany her to the doctor that afternoon. But David broke in.

"That's good," he said. "You have to go to a lot of psychiatrists to find one who won't try to throw you straight into a hospital."

It occurred to me that David's basic assumption was that if anybody needed a psychiatrist, it was not Mary but her father; not he but his mother. All straights worry David. A man who wears a coat and tie and has his hair cut short is obviously in need of help.

"David," I said, "this is a very serious matter. We have gone to a doctor. The doctor advises strongly that Mary enter a hospital at once. I believe in taking the advice of doctors. Now, will you help me?"

"Didn't I tell you, Dad?" said David. "Isn't that exactly what I said? Mary should go to a hospital if she wants to go to a hospital. I'll tell her that. But I won't tell her to go just because some psychiatrist said she should."

I called the doctor and told him to cancel the hospital room.

But what would happen to Mary, this intense and beautiful girl with the bright smile and the Phi Beta Kappa grades who wanted so much to do well at everything and always had?

Did I push her too hard? I remember telling her once that she ought to have more fun. Imagine, going to a college and not even knowing whether it had a football team. I did tell her that she studied too hard. But did I ever do anything to see that she did have fun? That bottle of wine she brought me from California—I put it away and said we'd go on a picnic one day and drink it, just the two of us. That was three years ago, and the wine—I knew where it lay in the cellar.

Not enough. That's what I did for Mary. Not enough. And what should I do now? I wished Mrs. Clark would come home.

Self-pity turns easily to anger, as I've often found when Joan is away. But this time, it seemed to me, I had just cause. "What the hell," I asked myself as the weeks went by, "does she think she is doing blithely flitting around Upper Volta, doubtless smiling at natives, leaving me here with a whole lot of children, one of whom is ill with an illness I don't understand?"

Blithe. It is a word I find helpful when I am angry at my wife, for it is true that she turns a blithe face to the world. Seat her at dinner next to a man with a reputation for taciturnity and you will shortly observe the most animated and sprightly of conversations. She is polite to the surly, soft-answered to the wrathful. She smiles at people on streets and says "Thank you" to startled elevator operators, disgorging passengers at the rush hour.

"That little freckle-faced girl," Jackie Kennedy once remarked to me, "does everything and goes everywhere and Jack and Bobby are forever asking her opinion and she has six [as it was then] children. Tell me, Tom, what is it about her?"

"Well, I'll tell you, Jackie, what it is about her. She's blithe. That's what it is about her, and that's why she is so everlastingly cheerful. What she needs is somebody to shake her by the shoulders and tell her that life is real and life is earnest and to quit smiling about it so much."

I didn't say that to Jackie's face. I said it to her when I was alone in my own room the evening after Mary had behaved strangely and the family conference had failed and the doctor had canceled the hospital room and Joan was in Upper Volta.

Sometime before Joan got home from Upper Volta, Mary found a very young, very long-haired psychiatrist who wore a sweater with a hole in the sleeve instead of a white jacket, and a beard instead of a mustache. But I was still annoyed with Joan, and never really got over being annoyed until last Labor Day.

When I woke up that morning, Mary was sitting as usual at the foot of the bed, waiting to talk to her mother. The moment she returned from Upper Volta, Joan initiated a series of conversations with Mary. They began each morning almost as soon as we awoke, and they seemed to me interminable.

I would shave and get dressed. Striding through the room, I would hear Mary say, "Do you think that Dad . . .?"

"Do you think," I would interrupt, "that Dad what?"

"Quiet, Tom," Joan would say, "Mary and I are talking."

So on Labor Day morning, there was Mary again on the edge of the bed, waiting. Mary, it seemed to me, was changing her personality. From participant to observer, from leader to follower, from active to passive. She had, quite suddenly, become timorous, shy, uncertain. Above all, she had become silent. Days would pass and except for the conversations with her mother, she would not utter a word. Psychiatrists do not talk to fathers. Mrs. Clark didn't say much either. I worried.

So I got out of bed and started to the bathroom to shave, and Joannie came in. Joannie was crying, "Mom, I can't tell two roommates that I'm dropping out. It's not fair."

Joannie was in a financial jam. She had signed up for an off-campus room at college and she didn't have the extra two hundred and eighty dollars.

Mrs. Clark held firm. "When you don't have the money, that's what you have to do."

I felt sorry for Joannie. It is difficult to say "No" to one who has brought gaiety and joy to the household all summer, who has planted flowers and cultivated them and brought them in in the morning with a joyful smile, saying, "Look."

And difficult to turn your back on one who has found herbs and searched the town for whole grains and had fun cooking "earth meals." More difficult when she is crying.

But Mrs. Clark was absolutely right. Joannie could have earned the extra money this past summer and she hadn't. So.

I finished shaving and walked back into the bedroom. Mary was still there, and Tommy was bouncing up and down on the bed, menacing Joan's coffee. "Careful, be careful, Tommy."

Elizabeth entered on cartwheels, beautiful, perfect cartwheels, legs straight up in the air at the top of the circle, long red hair mopping the floor. Joannie was still weeping silently and Mary waiting and Tommy bouncing and Mrs. Clark said to Elizabeth, "I called the school and they'll let you back in."

Everybody stopped. Everybody knew that Elizabeth had been expelled "for possession" and everybody was interested and considered Elizabeth to be wronged.

I was not sure she had been wronged. I "considered" her wronged, partly out of loyalty to Elizabeth and partly, as I told the school principal when he called, because there was no way of proving whether she was wrong or wronged.

She had passed a package of marijuana from one girl to the next on the school stairway, and when accosted had maintained that she did not know what she was passing.

Nicholas stormed in, wearing bright red pajamas. Joan made room for him under the covers. "Well, there you are."

And at once became Mrs. Clark again. "I told the principal," she said to Elizabeth, "that I didn't see any point in putting you on restrictions for violating the rules because obviously you know now what will happen to you if you violate rules."

One up for Mrs. Clark. She had reminded Elizabeth about rules without accusing her of breaking them; she had warned Elizabeth under pretext of defending her.

I went downstairs to boil myself an egg. There was, after all, a lot to be said for Joan. There she was up there with five people in her bedroom— one in money trouble, one in psychological trouble, one in disciplinary trouble, a fourth using her bed as a trampoline and a fifth wanting to be cuddled. Odd, the telephone hadn't rung. Usually it does, and Joan answers as gladly as though the one thing she had been missing was an offer of human companionship.

But today was Labor Day. People were not doing customary things. Susan, for example. She had already been out fishing and when she came in, she sat down at the table while I ate my egg. "What's up?" I asked casually.

"Thoreau is up," said Susan. "Thoreau on civil disobedience. I have to write a paper before I go back to school. Inviolability of the human spirit; the state can seize your body but cannot touch your mind. Get it?"

And just as I was about to say, "Yes, I get it," a voice interrupted. It was a pleasant voice, but firm. "Nonsense," said the voice, "if you get it, you get it wrong. Thoreau was a romantic. Read Orwell. Read *1984*. When the state held the rat in front of the man's face, the state seized his mind."

Susan and I looked in the direction of the voice. Mary was standing in the doorway.

I didn't say anything. I don't remember that Susan said anything. I remember that I looked at Susan and Susan looked at me, and both our mouths were open.

I went to the foot of the stairs and I called up to Mrs. Clark. "Joan," I said, "let's you and me go out to dinner tonight."

Blithe. That's the word. I felt absolutely blithe.

So Help Us, God

One winter little Joannie and I made an irregular practice of attending meetings of the Friends on Sunday mornings. Joannie had done some previous shopping around among local churches and had decided that the Friends were the best because various people were moved from time to time to say a word or two, and what they said was often thoughtful and interesting. There were no sermons.

We stopped going to the meetings because of an incident one Sunday, which both of us thought —in Joannie's words—was "dumb."

It was the first Sunday after Mr. Nixon's "incursion" into Cambodia and during the meditation a woman who wore a long gray hand-knitted shawl rose to suggest that those assembled ponder the devastation and the killing. For some days I had been musing upon the word "incursion," a new euphemism in the political language which seemed to me worthy of joining George Orwell's list of those words and phrases most often used to defend the indefensible: "transfer of population," "pacification."

"Latin words," wrote Orwell, "fall upon the facts like soft snow, blurring all the outlines and covering up the details. Millions of peasants are robbed of their farms and sent trudging along the roads with no more than they can carry. This is called rectification of frontiers."

"Incursion," I was reflecting, as the woman in the shawl spoke, had a clean, surgical sound, as in "Stand still now. This is going to hurt for *just* a minute." Who could hear the word "incursion" and picture the dust and the devastation, tanks leveling straw huts and the bombing of neutral people?

But immediately as the woman in the shawl subsided, a group seated up front rose huffily and departed. One of its members, a tall man, chesterfield-coated, wearing also, I noted, a vest and chain, remarked aloud that "Politics profanes a meeting house."

Those who remained appeared to side with the critics. The silence suddenly became embarassing and the woman in the shawl seemed very much alone.

Silently, Joannie and I took her part. What, we speculated on the way home, was the use of God if not to call upon when in trouble? And if the trouble was political, what difference, so long as it was personal too?

The only limitation on prayer, Joannie suggested

on the way home, should be the test of humanity. That is, no one should be permitted to pray for brutality, cruelty or unkindness.

I said I would add the test of sincerity and I told her the story of my Uncle Ray, who came to our house once a year when my father and his brothers held a reunion in our living room.

The reason they came to our town was that two of the brothers lived there—my father and my Uncle Baird, who was the minister of the First Baptist Church. The reason they came to our house instead of to Uncle Baird's was that all of the brothers except my father were ministers of various denominations, and so my father's house was a neutral ground. Uncle Baird, who was the oldest brother, always insisted upon leading the rest of them in prayer at these annual reunions, and I know my father was embarrassed each time.

But Uncle Baird cared and so my father did it. Mother would draw the blinds so that the living room was quite dark, and she would draw the curtain which separated the living room from the dining room. Though I was not admitted to the meeting, I knew that they were on their knees in there and I could hear Uncle Baird in prayer. Somehow, I shared my father's embarrassment, and if it had not been for my tall Uncle Ray, who was a Presbyterian minister from Oklahoma, I would be embarrassed still, and probably unable to relate the story to Joannie.

But Uncle Ray had his older brother pretty well fixed and I remember that when they had finished their meeting—and after Mother had drawn the curtain back—Uncle Ray would hold up his right hand and look straight at my father and would say, "Brothers, let us thank the Lord for this opportunity to have met once again and let us go out and do the work of the Lord, each of us in our own way, and Baird in his."

My father loved this old story and used to tell it long after Uncle Baird was dead. But I think the memory is one of the reasons why prayer in our family has never been public and the only occasions when any of us have mentioned the name of the Lord aloud have been those occasions when we needed Him, quick.

"Dad, Dad," I remember Nancy shouting. "Come now! It's Joannie!" I had told Joannie not to go out on the roof of the house to sunbathe, but I had not known that there was a skylight on the roof, else I might have told her in even stronger tones. The skylight was an old one and the glass had not been reinforced and now Joannie was protruding halfway through it, her legs bleeding horribly from the jagged wounds.

Quick action may have helped, and strength in my arms and knowing the way to the hospital and towels to staunch the bleeding. But I also think that saying over and over, "Oh, God, please. Oh, God, please," may have helped too, because that was one thing I did and everything I did must have been right to do. For Joannie recovered. Today her scars are not bad; perhaps some day they will be invisible.

"Is that a porpoise?" I asked Joan, as we were strolling on the beach. What I was looking at was a long way up the beach, exactly, I noticed, in front of our house. Joan couldn't see it. "Look," I said, pointing, "it's something tumbling in the waves, back and forth, and it looks like a baby porpoise, except—" And then I said, "My God! It's a white nightgown! It's Nancy!"

Near the water, where the sand is wet and hard, Oceanside's beach was very good for running, and I ran as fast as I could, which in those days was pretty fast. And all the time I ran, the "Please, God" tumbled over and over in my head. There is no doubt about it. God saved Nancy.

Certainly, I didn't save her. She'd obviously been tumbling back and forth in the waves for some time before I reached her, and a one-year-old child who has crawled into the sea survives, so it seems to me, only through the grace of God.

Surely, the same is true of four-year-olds on crowded freeways. We had taken two cars to drive back from Lake Tahoe and I was driving the second car, jammed with the used paraphernalia of a two-week vacation. David drove with me but Joan and the younger children were somewhere up in front, two or three miles, I estimated, remembering that she had pulled out first from the last stop for gasoline.

It had been a long, hot, silent ride through lonely country but now, as we approached Riverside at rush hour, the traffic boomed, with trucks and trailers and passenger cars all making the seventy-mile-per-hour limit in three fast lanes. Suddenly, there was a slowing down and a squawling of brakes, and the big truck in front of me flashed red signals and the driver had his hand out the window, palm outstretched for a stop.

Slowly now, we ground—the truck ahead in low gear—to the scene of whatever was holding up the long lines and then I saw a yellow dress and standing on the divider strip was Joan, the children around her, wide-eyed with fear, and in Joan's arms a bleeding mess.

Out, and onto the pavement and the bleeding mess was Nicholas, and a Mexican-looking man with a red half truck was shouting the way to the hospital and when I looked at him, helpless and confused, he said he'd lead me there.

I called out orders. David into the driver's seat of the first car. Everybody in that car home: Joan and I and the bloody mess—and then Elizabeth, whom David had forgotten in the confusion, squeezed in with the paraphernalia and we drove off the freeway, following the half truck to the hospital.

It was only then that I remarked that the bloody mess was screaming, "Oh, God, help me!" at the top of his lungs, over and over, unceasingly. "So he must be all right," I prayed to myself, and in fact, God must have remarked him too—and just in time.

Joan had been driving along at seventy miles an hour, and noting that home was barely an hour away, she had suggested that Nicky and Tommy clean up the back seat. Gum wrappers and other oddments on the floor were to go into the ashtrays next to the door latches. The door had flown open (it was one of those rear doors which open from the forward end of the car, so the wind can take control) and then Nicholas was hanging for a moment and then he wasn't.

One of the children told me later that he had bounced, in front of trucks and speeding cars, down the road a bit and then from the inside fast lane he bounced across two other lanes and into the brambles on the highway shoulder.

Only a four-year-old could have done it without breaking bones and even a four-year-old would have hit a wheel had it not been for God.

Nicholas' skin was pretty well frayed but otherwise there was nothing wrong with him whatever, and about four o'clock that morning he stopped crying out "God, help me" and went to sleep. Slowly the next morning, we proceeded, speculating, and giving thanks.

Nicholas seems to be accident-prone. When he was two, a girl whom Joan had hired "to help out" left him in the bathtub with the hot water running while she went to answer the telephone. It must have been more than a cursory conversation because by the time she got back, Nicholas was pretty well boiled and Mary, holding him while she called Dr. Harvey's office, noticed that his skin was coming off.

I think Stub Harvey was the one who saved Nicholas' life on that occasion, because he dropped whatever he was doing in his office, picked up Nicholas at the front door and had the treatment well under way at the hospital before Joan and I got there.

But maybe God was the one who presided over the unspoken pact of friendship which existed between Stub Harvey and me so that he was always ready and always on the run.

And surely God saved Nicholas' eyesight the time he got hit in the head with a baseball bat and I was out mowing the lawn, and grabbed him and rushed him to the hospital, bleeding from the eyes. Much as he was hurt, he refused to tell me the truth about what happened. "I fell down," he repeated. "Falling down," I chided him, "on your eyes?" "Yes," said Nicholas.

Nicholas protects to this day the name of the boy who accidently hit him with a baseball bat. The doctor said he had a fifty-fifty chance of losing his sight in both eyes, and that we would know after he had gone to bed for two weeks with bandages over them. Nicholas got the message, though he was only eight.

That afternoon, before the bandages were to go on, he walked around the house and in the yard and looked and looked with his one good eye. "So I can remember," he said, and then again, "God, help me." The rest of us cried a little and prayed that God would.

He always has. Some of that which He has done for our family, I probably do not know. Logic tells me that the older children must have been engaged in scrapes and narrow escapes which they have failed to report, except to Him.

Eight is too many to bring up without the help of God, but God must feel a little pressed sometimes when He hears our cries. I wonder whether the narrow escapes suggest that He too thinks eight is enough.

Fathers Can't Resign

I conclu
s belong

Fathers Can't Resign

There was a large dog mess on the front hall rug when Joan and I came in from a movie last night, and when Joan went upstairs with a weary sigh of resignation, she discovered another just outside our bedroom door. I went into the kitchen to turn the lights out. The floor was not quite ankle deep in trash.

"Now, let me explain about this. Trash goes into a large green plastic bag under the sink and each night the large green bag must be taken outdoors, placed in a container, and the lid securely fastened.

"You know that, don't you? Let me remind you why you know it. You know it because you know that if we leave the trash in the kitchen and somebody lets a dog in, the dog will tear the large green plastic bag into bits and strew the paper and the peeling and the tin cans all over the floor.

"Don't we both know that? Then, by God, why don't our children know it? And why do I have to be the one to cope with this goddamned mess?"

Some such speech—I think it was very nearly exactly that speech—was the speech I made to Joan last night, and as I concluded, an idea struck me and I acted at once before Joan could intervene.

"Just for once," I said, "I'm damned if I *will* cope with this goddamned mess," and I went upstairs, wakened each separately sleeping child and summoned him or her to duty.

There was, of course, an outcry, mostly from Tommy and Nicky, both of whom expressed their confidence that the dog—whichever dog it had been—had not been their dog. "It's not my fault," Nicholas said. "It wasn't my dog," said Tommy.

Nancy was harder to awaken, and when she arrived in the hall she said she thought I was crazy. Mary and Elizabeth suggested, without quite saying so, that they agreed. By the time everyone had expressed an opinion, the dog messes had been cleaned up and the kitchen floor too.

It was all over in less than fifteen minutes. But there had been, as Joan pointed out when we reached the bedroom, a certain emotional cost. "If you keep this up, you will have a heart attack."

"No," I replied, "I will not have a heart attack. I will have children who realize their responsibilities."

How many years have I been saying that? How many more years will there be? The face of my friend the beautiful Elizabeth Weymouth came

to mind, and I saw her laughing at me, then saying, quite seriously, "You really are a little bit
of a fool."

The beautiful Elizabeth Weymouth had been
visiting us in Oceanside, and there had been a
large beach party in honor of her and her two
tiny children. Many children had come as guests
and run up and down from the kitchen to the sand
on the beach and back again. Before I went to
bed, I scrubbed the kitchen floor.

Next morning, first to rise, I found it deep in
grape juice, the linoleum still sparkling under the
dark purple, like a coral bottom to a smooth sea.
But as I stood at the kitchen door and gazed
with mingled shock and sorrow, I noted a small
flaw upon the surface of the sea. It was right in
front of the refrigerator. Was it a smudge? Was
it a high place in the linoleum? Was it half a
slice of bread? No. It was a footprint. Clearly, it
was a footprint, a small footprint, but not a tiny
footprint, not the footprint of a visiting child.
This was the footprint of Nicholas, or it was the
footprint of Tommy, one or the other, it had to be.

And so, I fetched them from their rooms while
they protested loudly, and I held them up over
the kitchen floor, Tommy in his pajamas, Nicholas
in his pajamas, bare foot of Nicholas against the
print; bare foot of Tommy against the print. And
I was standing there in the grape juice, holding
Tommy over the footprint when I looked up, to
find the beautiful Elizabeth Weymouth watching
me from the kitchen door.

"A little bit of a fool." How many more years

would I go on being a little bit of a fool? Or did I have to go on? Was this last business—this getting all the children out of bed to clean up dog messes—was that again the mark of a fool?

I got into bed and picked up a book, but my mind unaccountably conjured up that moment in the hotel room when I had resigned as a father.

Once again, I heard Joan's voice over the noise of the aircraft engines: "I can see both sides." Once again, I saw the look of disdain on Mary's face, and once again I heard her words: "You act as though you were some kind of platoon leader. Don't you think running things as though we were all in the army is a little bit, shall I say, old-fashioned?"

That resignation, I now reflected, had been an enormously pleasurable experience, rather like having a shot of Demerol when in pain. I lay back and let the scene replay itself in my mind.

First, I had sorted out the remains of each airplane ticket. Then, stepping over the clothes and the bedding in three hotel rooms, I had made delivery, each to each. Quite seriously, and without a hint of either sorrow or anger, I had said to each child as I handed over each ticket: "I am resigning as your father effective right now."

I had paid no attention to retorts. Someone said, "Oh, Dad." Another, I think, said something which might have been interpreted as apologetic. I do not remember. I did not really listen. I had made up my mind. "Joan," I said casually when I was dressed and ready and had packed my bag, "let's go down to the lobby and get a taxi; we can just catch the eleven o'clock home."

There had been consternation and the consternation had been pleasant too. Forewarned by the delivery of the tickets, they had all gathered in our room. Elizabeth had asked the question which gave me an opening for a parting shot. "If you and Mom go, Dad, who's going to pay the cab drivers?"

"You might ask Mary that question," I answered. "She may want to take a vote so that you won't all feel as though you're in the army."

A second parting shot occurred. "Nancy will pay. She has her own money."

For a moment, I really had resigned. I had pretended that I didn't care and, for a moment, the pretense was reality. It would not be up to me any more. I would not have to worry about their tickets or their suitcases or their money or whether there were boys in their rooms, or whether one of them was out at night on a bicycle or what time they got in or about the causes of the Civil War. There would be only Joan. It would be quiet. It would be peaceful. It would be inexpensive, My God, how inexpensive it would be.

Somewhere I have read that four out of ten American marriages now end in divorce, and a reporter for a national news magazine had discovered that the reason for divorce most often given by those who were about to undertake it was, "When the children began to grow up, I couldn't stand them any more."

It would be different without children. I would be carefree, gay, young. And ,oan. She too would be carefree. That little worried frown she sometimes gets between her eyebrows; it would go, and so would that persevering look she occasionally wears. Her face would fill out and she would look as she did when she and I were young.

And so I lay there, in bed, holding the book I wasn't reading and recapturing the moment of my resignation, savoring it, pretending how it would be if that moment had been the end. But the reel of memory had begun. There was no stopping it. The scene played on.

There they were, all assembled in Joan's and my room, standing or sitting between me and two unmade beds. They were dressed and ready and waiting. Outside the open door, I could see the bags, lined up neatly against the wall of the corridor opposite, lined up neatly for the first time on that journey, by someone other than me.

There was David, my red-haired oldest son, rightfully holding all the tickets I had individually handed out earlier, looking at me with a wise, half-amused smile. There were Nicholas and Tommy, the two youngest boys, wearing their blue suits, properly buttoned. Their hair had been brushed, and their eyes were wide and questioning.

And there were the girls—Mary viewing me, I thought with conscious tolerance; Joannie, Susan, Nancy and Elizabeth waiting for me to make a move.

I picked up Joan's bag with one hand, grabbing my own in the other and gesturing with my head toward the door. "Joan, let's go."

As I did so, Joan's eyes caught mine and I knew she knew the truth. But I strode ahead, down the hall toward the elevator, carrying a bag in each hand, feigning oblivion to the sound of other suitcases being picked up and of an army scrambling after.

And then my heart had suddenly swollen with that mixture of pride and affection, protectiveness and hope which is, I now reflected, what makes a father go on being a father. What is a father for?

To make sure that his children have a chance to play their parts. I guess that's what a father is for: to do his best to see that they grow up to be worthy of trust in whatever kind of world they're going to live in.

Is that what I want? I think so. "But it may be," I said to myself that night as I thought about the resignation, "that what I really want is to see how it all comes out."

Anyhow, you can't resign. Halfway down the long hall which led to the elevator, I turned and retraced my steps, passing the line of struggling stragglers on the way. At the end was small Nicholas, his back turned toward his objective, his arms outstretched, pulling his suitcase along the hotel carpet. I put one of my bags under my left arm, took his suitcase in my right hand and strode back toward the elevator. "We'll need two cabs," I said to David, as I passed him, "two cabs, as usual."